SAFETY AND RISK IN SOCIETY

FEDERAL CYBERSECURITY PLANNING:

HUMAN CAPITAL AND RESEARCH AND DEVELOPMENT

SAFETY AND RISK IN SOCIETY

Additional books in this series can be found on Nova's website under the Series tab.

Additional E-books in this series can be found on Nova's website under the E-books tab.

DEFENSE, SECURITY AND STRATEGIES

Additional books in this series can be found on Nova's website under the Series tab.

Additional E-books in this series can be found on Nova's website under the E-books tab.

CONTENTS

Preface vii

Chapter 1 Cybersecurity Human Capital: Initiatives Need
Better Planning and Coordination 1
United States Government Accountability Office

Chapter 2 Cybersecurity: Key Challenges Need to Be
Addressed to Improve Research and Development 65
United States Government Accountability Office

Index 95

PREFACE

Threats to federal information technology (IT) infrastructure and systems continue to grow in number and sophistication. The ability to make federal IT infrastructure and systems secure depends on the knowledge, skills, and abilities of the federal and contractor workforce that implements and maintains these systems. In light of the importance of recruiting and retaining cybersecurity personnel, this book examines the extent to which federal agencies have implemented and established workforce planning practices for cybersecurity personnel and explores the status of and plans for government-wide cybersecurity workforce initiatives.

Chapter 1 - Threats to federal information technology (IT) infrastructure and systems continue to grow in number and sophistication. The ability to make federal IT infrastructure and systems secure depends on the knowledge, skills, and abilities of the federal and contractor workforce that implements and maintains these systems.

In light of the importance of recruiting and retaining cybersecurity personnel, GAO was asked to assess (1) the extent to which federal agencies have implemented and established workforce planning practices for cybersecurity personnel and (2) the status of and plans for governmentwide cybersecurity workforce initiatives.

GAO evaluated eight federal agencies with the highest IT budgets to determine their use of workforce planning practices for cybersecurity staff by analyzing plans, performance measures, and other information. GAO also reviewed plans and programs at agencies with responsibility for government wide cybersecurity workforce initiatives.

Chapter 2 - Computer networks and infrastructures, on which the United States and much of the world rely to communicate and conduct business, contain vulnerabilities that can leave them susceptible to unauthorized access, disruption, or attack. Investing in research and development (R&D) is essential to protect critical systems and to enhance the cybersecurity of both the government and the private sector. Federal law has called for improvements in cybersecurity R&D, and, recently, President Obama has stated that advancing R&D is one of his administration's top priorities for improving cybersecurity.

GAO was asked to determine the key challenges in enhancing national-level cybersecurity R&D efforts among the federal government and private companies. To do this, GAO consulted with officials from relevant federal agencies and experts from private sector companies and academic institutions as well as analyzed key documents, such as agencies' research plans.

In: Federal Cybersecurity Planning
Editors: K. C. Moore and M. D. Taylor
ISBN 978-1-61942-769-3
© 2012 Nova Science Publishers, Inc.

Chapter 1

CYBERSECURITY HUMAN CAPITAL: INITIATIVES NEED BETTER PLANNING AND COORDINATION[*]

United States Government Accountability Office

WHY GAO DID THIS STUDY

Threats to federal information technology (IT) infrastructure and systems continue to grow in number and sophistication. The ability to make federal IT infrastructure and systems secure depends on the knowledge, skills, and abilities of the federal and contractor workforce that implements and maintains these systems.

In light of the importance of recruiting and retaining cybersecurity personnel, GAO was asked to assess (1) the extent to which federal agencies have implemented and established workforce planning practices for cybersecurity personnel and (2) the status of and plans for governmentwide cybersecurity workforce initiatives.

GAO evaluated eight federal agencies with the highest IT budgets to determine their use of workforce planning practices for cybersecurity staff by analyzing plans, performance measures, and other information. GAO also

---

[*] This is an edited, reformatted and augmented version of a United States Government Accountability Office Report to the Chairman, Subcommittee on Immigration, GAO-12-8 dated November 2011.

reviewed plans and programs at agencies with responsibility for government-wide cybersecurity workforce initiatives.

WHAT GAO RECOMMENDS

GAO is making recommendations to enhance individual agency cybersecurity workforce planning activities and to address governmentwide cybersecurity workforce challenges through better planning, coordination, and evaluation of govern mentwide activities. Agencies concurred with the majority of GAO's recommendations and outlined steps to address them. Two agencies did not provide comments on the report.

WHAT GAO FOUND

Federal agencies have taken varied steps to implement workforce planning practices for cybersecurity personnel. Five of eight agencies, including the largest, the Department of Defense, have established cybersecurity workforce plans or other agencywide activities addressing cybersecurity workforce planning. However, all of the agencies GAO reviewed faced challenges determining the size of their cybersecurity workforce because of variations in how work is defined and the lack of an occupational series specific to cybersecurity. With respect to other workforce planning practices, all agencies had defined roles and responsibilities for their cybersecurity workforce, but these roles did not always align with guidelines issued by the federal Chief Information Officers Council and National Institute of Standards and Technology (NIST). Agencies reported challenges in filling highly technical positions, challenges due to the length and complexity of the federal hiring process, and discrepancies in compensation across agencies. Although most agencies used some form of incentives to support their cybersecurity workforce, none of the eight agencies had metrics to measure the effectiveness of these incentives. Finally, the robustness and availability of cybersecurity training and development programs varied significantly among the agencies. For example, the Departments of Commerce and Defense required cybersecurity personnel to obtain certifications and fulfill continuing education requirements. Other agencies used an informal or ad hoc approach to identifying required training.

The federal government has begun several governmentwide initiatives to enhance the federal cybersecurity workforce. The National Initiative for Cybersecurity Education, coordinated by NIST, includes activities to examine and more clearly define the federal cybersecurity workforce structure and roles and responsibilities, and to improve cybersecurity workforce training. However, the initiative lacks plans defining tasks and milestones to achieve its objectives, a clear list of agency activities that are part of the initiative, and a means to measure the progress of each activity. The Chief Information Officers Council, NIST, Office of Personnel Management, and the Department of Homeland Security (DHS) have also taken steps to define skills, competencies, roles, and responsibilities for the federal cybersecurity workforce. However, these efforts overlap and are potentially duplicative, although officials from these agencies reported beginning to take steps to coordinate activities. Furthermore, there is no plan to promote use of the outcomes of these efforts by individual agencies. The Office of Management and Budget and DHS have identified several agencies to be service centers for governmentwide cybersecurity training, but none of the service centers or DHS currently evaluates the training for duplicative content, effectiveness, or extent of use by federal agencies. The Scholarship for Service program, run by the National Science Foundation, is a small though useful source of new talent for the federal government, but the program lacks data on whether its participants remain in the government long-term.

ABBREVIATIONS

CIO	Chief Information Officer
Commerce	Department of Commerce
DHS	Department of Homeland Security
DOD	Department of Defense
DOT	Department of Transportation
FBI	Federal Bureau of Investigation
FedCTE	Federal Cybersecurity Training Event
FISMA	Federal Information Security Management Act
FedVTE	Federal Virtual Training Environment
FTE	full time equivalent
GS	General Schedule
HHS	Department of Health and Human Services
IT	information technology

Justice	Department of Justice
NASA	National Aeronautics and Space Administration
NICE	National Initiative for Cybersecurity Education
NIST	National Institute of Standards and Technology
NSA	National Security Agency
NSF	National Science Foundation
OMB	Office of Management and Budget
OPM	Office of Personnel Management
SFS	Scholarship for Service
SP	Special Publication
State	Department of State
Treasury	Department of the Treasury
VA	Department of Veterans Affairs

November 29, 2011

The Honorable Charles E. Schumer Chairman
Subcommittee on Immigration, Refugees, and Border Security
Committee on the Judiciary
United States Senate

Dear Mr. Chairman:

Federal electronic information and infrastructure are under attack from both domestic and foreign attackers who wish to penetrate and harm our networks. Threats to federal information technology (IT) infrastructure continue to grow in number and sophistication, posing a risk to the reliable functioning of our government. Securing federal networks is an evolving challenge for many reasons, including the anonymity of the Internet and because of the ever-changing nature of technology. In discussing his 2009 Cyberspace Policy Review,[1] President Obama declared the cyber threat to be "One of the most serious economic and national security challenges we face as a nation." Since 1997, we have identified the protection of federal information systems as a high-risk area for the government.[2] Essential to protecting our information and infrastructure is having a resilient, well-trained, and dedicated cybersecurity workforce.

Accordingly, as agreed with your office, the objectives of our review were to assess (1) the extent to which key federal agencies have implemented established workforce planning practices for cybersecurity personnel and (2) the status of and plans for governmentwide cybersecurity workforce initiatives. To address the first objective, we reviewed information related to workforce planning at the eight federal agencies and their components that have the highest budgets for IT: the Departments of Defense (DOD), Homeland Security (DHS), Health and Human Services (HHS), Treasury, Veterans Affairs (VA), Commerce, Transportation (DOT), and Justice. We used this information to evaluate each agency's efforts to identify critical cybersecurity skills and competencies needed, challenges in developing or obtaining the skills and competencies, and plans to address the challenges based on leading practices in workforce planning. To address our second objective, at agencies and organizations with specific governmentwide cybersecurity responsibilities, such as the National Institute of Standards and Technology (N IST), the Office of Personnel Management (OPM), the federal Chief Information Officers (CIO) Council, DHS, the National Science Foundation (NSF), and the Office of Management and Budget (OMB), we assessed plans and other efforts to coordinate cybersecurity workforce initiatives against leading practices in program management.

We conducted this performance audit at the agencies previously named in and around Washington, D.C., from December 2010 to November 2011, in accordance with generally accepted government auditing standards. Those standards require that we plan and perform the audit to obtain sufficient, appropriate evidence to provide a reasonable basis for our findings and conclusions based on our audit objectives. We believe that the evidence obtained provides a reasonable basis for our findings and conclusions based on our audit objectives. Further details on our objectives, scope, and methodology are contained in appendix I.

BACKGROUND

Federal agencies have become increasingly dependent on electronic networks to carry out their operations. Virtually all federal operations are supported by automated systems and electronic data, and agencies would find it difficult, if not impossible, to carry out their missions, deliver services to the public, and account for their resources without these electronic information assets. The security of these systems is especially important to ensure the confidentiality, integrity, and availability of the information that resides on them. Conversely, ineffective information security can result in significant risk to a broad array of government operations and assets. Specifically,

- Resources, such as federal payments and collections, could be lost or stolen.
- Computer resources could be used for unauthorized purposes or to launch attacks on other computer systems.
- Sensitive information, such as taxpayer data, Social Security records, medical records, intellectual property, and proprietary business information, could be inappropriately disclosed, browsed, or copied for purposes of identity theft, espionage, or other types of crime.
- Critical operations, such as those supporting critical infrastructure, financial systems, national defense, and emergency services, could be exploited, disrupted, or destroyed.

Because of the importance of federal information systems to government operations, and because of continuing weaknesses in the information security controls over these systems, we have identified federal information security as a governmentwide high-risk area since 1997.[3]

Threats to federal information systems can be internal or external, accidental or targeted. They can range from individual hackers looking to do some mischief to terrorists or organized, state-sponsored groups looking to steal information or launch a cyber attack to cripple critical infrastructure. Recently, the Commander of the U.S. Cyber Command stated that "even the most astute malicious cyber actors—those who can break into almost any network that they really try to penetrate—are usually searching for targets of opportunity. They search for easy vulnerabilities in our systems' security and then exploit them."[4]

Cybersecurity professionals help to prevent or mitigate these vulnerabilities that could allow malicious individuals and groups access to federal IT systems. Specifically, the ability to secure federal systems is dependent on the knowledge, skills, and abilities of the federal and contractor workforce that uses, implements, secures, and maintains these systems. This includes federal and contractor employees who use the IT systems in the course of their work and the designers, developers, programmers, and administrators of the programs and systems.

Several organizations have identified challenges facing the federal cybersecurity workforce. In July 2009, the Partnership for Public Service[5] reported challenges to maintaining the quality and quantity of the federal cybersecurity workforce, including the following:

- Federal cybersecurity workforce planning and decision making is decentralized across agencies.
- Agencies cannot readily identify the size of their cybersecurity workforce.
- Complicated rules and processes hamper recruiting and retention efforts.

In 2010, the Center for Strategic and International Studies reported[6] a shortage of qualified cybersecurity professionals in the United States, including those who can design secure systems, write secure computer code, and create the tools needed to prevent, detect, mitigate, and reconstitute information systems. According to the report, an organization's cybersecurity strategy should

- use hiring, acquisition, and training to raise the level of technical competence of those who build, operate, and protect government systems;
- establish a career path that rewards and retains those with the appropriate technical skills; and
- support development and adoption of rigorous technical certifications.

Within the federal government, others have identified cybersecurityrelated workforce challenges at federal agencies. In September 2009, the Department of Commerce Inspector General reported that the department needed to devote more attention to the development and management of its cybersecurity personnel, and cited problems with training, performance management, and accountability of cybersecurity staff in the department.[7] In June 2010, the DHS Inspector General reported that difficulties filling vacant positions at the department's National Cyber Security Division were hampering its ability to achieve its mission.[8] In March 2011, the Commander of the U.S. Cyber Command testified that the military did not have enough highly skilled personnel to address the current and future cyber threats to our infrastructure.[9] Finally, in April 2011, the Inspector General at the Department of Justice reported that more than one-third of field agents interviewed for an audit reported that they lacked sufficient expertise to investigate the national security-related cyber intrusion cases that they had been assigned.[10]

AGENCIES VARY IN THEIR USE OF WORKFORCE PLANNING PRACTICES FOR CYBERSECURITY

Developing a strong workforce requires planning to acquire, develop, and retain it. Agency approaches to such planning can vary with the agency's particular needs and mission. Nevertheless, our own work and the work of other organizations, such as OPM,[11] suggest that there are leading practices that workforce planning should address, such as

- Developing workforce plans that link to the agency's strategic plan. Among other things, these plans should identify activities required to carry out the goals and objectives of the agency's strategic plan and include analysis of the current workforce to meet long-term and short-term goals and objectives.
- Identifying the type and number of staff needed for an agency to achieve its mission and goals.
- Defining roles, responsibilities, skills, and competencies for key positions.
- Developing strategies to address recruiting needs and barriers to filling cybersecurity positions.
- Ensuring compensation incentives and flexibilities are effectively used to recruit and retain employees for key positions.
- Ensuring compensation systems are designed to help the agency compete for and retain the talent it needs to attain its goals.
- Establishing a training and development program that supports the competencies the agency needs to accomplish its mission.

Development and Implementation of Workforce Plans that Link to Agency Strategic Plans and Define Cybersecurity Workforce Needs Vary by Agency

Preparing a strategic workforce plan encourages agency managers and stakeholders to systematically consider what is to be done, when and how it will be done, what skills will be needed, and how to gauge progress and results. In addition, as part of its Human Capital Assessment and Accountability Framework, OPM requires agencies to maintain a current human capital plan and submit an annual human capital accountability report.[12]

Agency approaches to such planning can vary with each agency's particular needs and mission. Nevertheless, existing strategic workforce planning tools and models and our own work suggest that there are key principles that such a process should address irrespective of the context in which the planning is done (see figure 1).

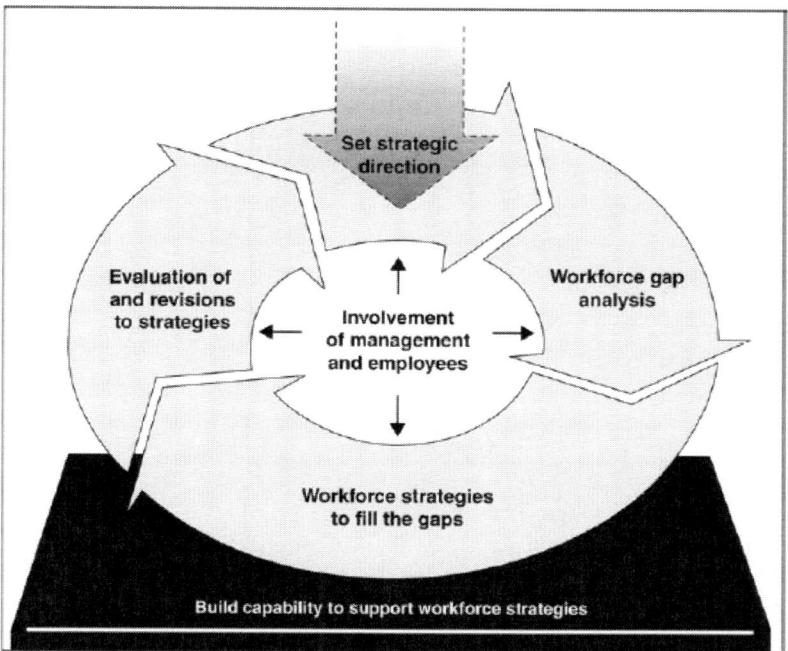

Source: GAO.

Figure 1. Strategic Workforce Planning Process.

These key principles to address strategic workforce planning are to[13]

- involve top management, employees, and other stakeholders in developing, communicating, and implementing the strategic workforce plan;
- determine the critical skills and competencies that will be needed to achieve current and future programmatic results;
- develop strategies that are tailored to address gaps in number, deployment, and alignment of human capital approaches for enabling and sustaining the contributions of all critical skills and competencies;

- build the capability needed to address administrative, educational, and other requirements important to support workforce strategies; and
- monitor and evaluate the agency's progress toward its human capital goals and the contribution that human capital results have made toward achieving programmatic goals.

Table 1. Key Principles Addressed by Agency Workforce Plans

Agency	Involve top management, employees, and other stakeholders	Determine critical skills and competencies	Develop strategies that are tailored to address gaps in human capital approaches and critical skills and competencies	Build the capability needed to address requirements to support workforce strategies	Monitor and evaluate the agency's progress
DOD	yes	yes	partial	partial	yes
DHS	yes	yes	yes	yes	yes
Justice	yes	yes	yes	yes	yes
DOT	yes	yes	partial	partial	yes
VA	no	yes	partial	no	partial

Source: GAO analysis of agency workforce plans.

Note: Commerce, HHS, and Treasury did not provide either departmentwide or cybersecurity specific workforce plans. DOD and DOT had workforce plans that specifically defined cybersecurity workforce needs.

Of the eight agencies we reviewed, two agencies, DOD and DOT have workforce plans that specifically define cybersecurity workforce needs. Two agencies DHS and Justice, have departmentwide workforce plans that, although not specific to cybersecurity, do address cybersecurity personnel. One agency VA, has a guide on implementing competency models[14] that addresses elements of workforce planning, although it has neither a cybersecurity nor a departmentwide workforce plan. The remaining three agencies Commerce, HHS, and Treasury have neither departmental workforce plans nor workforce plans that specifically address cybersecurity workforce needs. Regarding the agencies with workforce plans or a competency guide, table 1 illustrates which key principles were addressed.

DOD has an information assurance workforce plan that describes the involvement of representatives of top management including the Chairman of the Joint Chiefs of Staff, the Under Secretary of Defense for Intelligence, the

Defense Information Systems Agency, and the U.S. Strategic Command. The plan also incorporates critical skills, competencies, categories, and specialties of the information assurance workforce. However, the plan only partially describes strategies to address gaps in human capital approaches and critical skills and competencies. For example, the plan addresses gap analysis, education trends for the future IT workforce, identification and training of the current cybersecurity workforce, and recruitment and retention strategies. Additionally, the plan includes a timeline and goals to budget for, identify, train, and certify the DOD information assurance workforce over a 6-year period. However, the plan does not address performance management or recruiting flexibilities (e.g., alternative work schedules and special hiring authorities). In addition, the plan only partially describes building the capacity to support workforce strategies. Specifically, it states DOD will improve workforce processes, but does not discuss educating managers and employees on the use of recruiting flexibilities, having clear guidelines for using specific flexibilities, and holding managers and supervisors accountable for their effective use.

DHS has a departmentwide IT strategic human capital plan, although not a specific workforce plan for cybersecurity. The IT strategic human capital plan describes top management involvement and details workforce demographics and an IT occupational series that includes many of the department's cybersecurity positions. The plan also includes developing strategies to address workforce issues and states that DHS will develop IT competency models (including leadership competencies, project/program management, and others) that will identify behaviors, skills, and abilities needed to support DHS's mission requirements and provide a foundation for recruitment, career development, performance management, and employee recognition. The plan also discusses building the capacity to address requirements to support workforce strategies by improving workforce processes and developing metrics to assess human capital performance. In addition, the plan addresses the following objectives: IT talent acquisition and branding, IT employee development and retention, IT workforce performance, IT workforce capacity.

Similarly, Justice has a departmentwide workforce plan, although not a specific workforce plan for cybersecurity. The departmentwide plan includes evidence of senior management coordination among multiple department components. In addition, the plan identifies critical skills and workforce information such as projected requirements and strategies for addressing gaps for many occupations including that of information technology specialist, which includes many of the department's cybersecurity positions. The plan also discusses developing strategies to address workforce issues such as how Justice will use various efforts to build the workforce, including identifying future IT workforce competency and skill requirements and developing recruitment and training activities. Further, the plan addresses building the capacity to address requirements such as how Justice will develop programs and improve processes to grow a workforce that can achieve the goals and meet the current and future challenges of the department's mission. In addition, the plan states that Justice will develop innovative programs, improve performance and accountability, and focus on performance metrics and measures.

DOT has a cybersecurity strategic plan that addresses workforce issues. Specifically, the plan discusses involvement of the Office of the CIO and other business owners. It identifies and defines roles specific to information security, such as the roles for chief information security officer, systems operations and maintenance professional, and network security specialist. However, the plan only partially outlines developing strategies to address gaps in human capital approaches and critical skills and competencies. For example, it states that DOT will develop the workforce, including upgrading the skill sets of its technical workforce and improving on the general skill sets of DOT employees and contractors. The plan also addresses gaps in workforce number and performance. However, the plan does not discuss hiring flexibilities and succession planning. In addition, the plan only partially addresses elements of building the capacity to support workforce strategies since the plan does not address educating managers and employees on the availability and use of recruiting flexibilities.

Finally, VA has developed a competency model guide that agency officials stated was used for workforce planning, although the agency did not have a specific workforce plan for cybersecurity or a departmentwide workforce plan. The guide includes skills and competencies needed at the agency. However, it does not address the involvement of top management in workforce planning. In addition, the guide only partially addresses developing strategies to address gaps in human capital approaches and critical skills and competencies. Specifically, the guide discusses needed data calls and budget forecasts and the importance of offering clear career paths, training, and professional development for critical IT positions. However, the guide does not address hiring flexibilities and succession planning. Furthermore, it does not address building the capacity to address requirements to support workforce strategies such as educating managers on the availability and use of flexibilities, streamlining and improving administrative processes, or building accountability into the system. In addition, the guide only partially addresses how the department will monitor and evaluate the agency's progress toward its human capital goals. Specifically, the guide discusses tracking employee progress in training and completion of tasks, but does not specifically mention monitoring and evaluation of agency implementation of its workforce plan or the outcomes of its human capital strategies. At the conclusion of our review, the department reported that it was initiating a departmentwide effort to identify and address its workforce planning needs.

Three agencies—Commerce, HHS, and Treasury did not have a workforce plan for the department or one that specifically addressed cybersecurity workforce needs. These agencies reported different reasons for not having a cybersecurity workforce plan. For example, Commerce tracks cybersecurity workforce issues through reporting tools such as its balanced scorecard. The department stated it had defined necessary role-based training and skills for IT personnel with significant IT security roles and respon-sibilities. However, workforce planning is decentralized to its component organizations. The department provided evidence of steps it has been taking to oversee component cybersecurity workforce planning activities, such as recent compliance reviews, but acknowledged it did not have a detailed view of whether components were conducting workforce planning activities. At HHS, the Chief Information Security Officer stated that human capital requirements are determined by individual offices and are addressed during the department's budget development and justification process, and while the department has not formally defined the size of its cybersecurity workforce needs, it has documented plans for hiring, recruiting, and retaining personnel that map to recent OPM initiatives to streamline hiring. Finally, the Treasury Associate Chief Human Capital Officer indicated that workforce planning efforts are at the discretion of each of its component bureaus and stated that she believed the department's bureaus were performing the necessary workforce planning. At the conclusion of our audit, Treasury officials stated the department had formed a workforce planning group to standardize processes to better conduct agencywide workforce planning.

Our prior work has shown that a workforce plan can help agencies define human capital goals and measure progress toward those goals. While the exact structure and level of centralization of such a plan may vary by agency, having some form of centralized oversight is crucial to effective management and accountability. In August 2011, OMB explicitly singled out information security as a primary responsibility for agency CIOs at all federal agencies.[15] Until all agencies establish workforce plans to address cybersecurity or ensure that their components are establishing such a plan, the ability of the agency's CIO to ensure cybersecurity staff are able to support the agency's information security goals may be limited.

Agencies Have Difficulty Identifying the Size of Their Cybersecurity Workforce

Successful human capital management and workforce planning are dependent on having and using valid and reliable data. These data can help an agency determine performance objectives, goals, the appropriate number of employees, and develop strategies to address gaps in the number, deployment, and alignment of employees.

However, the agencies we reviewed do not have consistent data on the size of their cybersecurity workforce. Table 2 presents cybersecurity workforce data for these agencies from four different sources:

- Data gathered by OMB as part of its reporting requirements under the Federal Information Security Management Act (FISMA).[16] In March 2011, OMB reported the total number of full-time equivalents (FTEs)[17] with major information security responsibilities at the eight agencies we reviewed—both federal employees and contractors—was about 75,000. Of these, approximately 49,000 were federal FTEs and approximately 25,000 were contractor FTEs.
- The number of employees with significant information security responsibilities reported by each agency in its FISMA report for fiscal year 2010.
- Information gathered by OPM in 2010 as part of an informal data collection on the federal cybersecurity workforce. Six of the eight agencies we reviewed responded to OPM's data call, and in aggregate, they reported a total of about 35,000 workers engaged in cybersecurity work. However, it is not clear whether that number included the intelligence workforce and contractors.
- The results of our request to agencies to identify their number of cybersecurity employees.

The data provided vary widely based on specific data call requirements. For example, DOD reported about 87,000 FTEs with significant security responsibilities for its FISMA report, but just under 19,000 personnel in cybersecurity to OPM. VA was identified as having about 800 FTEs in OMB's FISMA report, but reported almost 9,900 personnel with significant security responsibilities in its agency FISMA report.

Table 2. Comparison of Reported Number of Cybersecurity Workers from Multiple Sources

Agency	FTEs per OMB's Fiscal Year 2010 FISMA report	Personnel reported in 2010 agency FISMA report of personnel with significant information security responsibilities	Personnel per OPM 2010 data gathering	Personnel per GAO 2011 data call
Commerce	1,161	1,258	not reported	373
DOD	66,000	87,846	18,955	88,159
HHS	965	6,244	16	not reported
DHS	1,453	3,350	12,500	1,361
Justice	2,887	2,989	2,632	283
DOT	524	848	not reported	not reported
Treasury	1,175	7,833	734	904
VA	836	9,887	400	not reported

Source: GAO analysis of OMB and agency reports and agency-provided data.
Note: The numbers in the table are estimations, and do not include intelligence personnel for several agencies, including DOD and Justice.

The difficulty in identifying the size of the cybersecurity workforce is partly due to the challenge of defining a cybersecurity worker. FISMA-related guidance asks federal agencies to track the number of personnel who have significant information security responsibilities and have received role-based security training each year. It is possible for an employee to perform a significant security responsibility, such as authorizing operation of a system, without that being the majority of his or her work. In addition, many employees may perform cybersecurity responsibilities as an additional duty and not as their primary job responsibility. During our review, we were asked by agencies to provide a more specific definition for cybersecurity staff, so we asked agencies to identify the number of employees who spend a majority of their time performing cybersecurity responsibilities.

Furthermore, there is no specific federal occupational series that identifies federal cybersecurity positions. A series is used to identify a specific occupation and generally includes all jobs in that particular kind of work at all grade levels. Many agencies use the occupational series developed by OPM. However, OPM's 2010 cybersecurity data collection showed that federal agencies used multiple series for their cybersecurity workforce. (See table 3.)

Table 3. Occupational Series Commonly Used for Cybersecurity Workforce

Occupational series	Series group name
0080	Security administration series
0132	Intelligence series
0301	Miscellaneous administration and program series
0340	Program management series
0391	Telecommunications series
0801	General engineering series
0854	Computer engineering series
0855	Electronic engineering series
1101	General business and industry series
1301	General physical science series
1550	Computer science series
1801	General inspection, investigation, enforcement, and compliance series
1805	Investigative analysis series
1810	General investigation series
1811	Criminal investigation series
2010	Inventory management series
2210	Information technology management series

Source: GAO summary, based on OPM's responses and General Schedule.

None of these series identifies cybersecurity as the only job responsibility. In many cases, employees with cybersecurity responsibilities also have other responsibilities, and some employees classified under a particular series may not have any cybersecurity responsibilities.

The 2210 series, information technology management, has a parenthetical title, a form of subclassification, which can be used to identify information security positions. Six of the eight agencies we reviewed primarily used this series for their cybersecurity workforce. However, the parenthetical title is not used consistently at the federal agencies we reviewed.

Even within an agency there is inconsistency in defining cybersecurity positions. For example, we previously reported[18] that DOD lacked a common definition for cybersecurity personnel among the different services, which created challenges in determining adequate types and numbers of cybersecurity personnel.

While several agency officials stated that a single occupational series for cybersecurity would make collecting information on their cybersecurity workforce easier, both they and OPM identified additional problems this could create in not accurately reflecting the noncybersecurity work that a particular employee may perform, and in limiting an employee's career mobility. As a result, although OPM officials stated that currently there is no way other than creating an occupational series to allow easy identification of cybersecurity employees governmentwide, OPM is not planning to create such a job series. They stated that determining a way to track federal cybersecurity personnel is to be part of future efforts to reform federal personnel systems, but did not yet have specific milestones or tasks for doing so.

The difficulties in identifying the cybersecurity workforce mean that most of the agencies we reviewed rely on manual processes to gather information on their workforce. Only two of the eight agencies we reviewed—Commerce and Treasury—were able to use an automated agencywide process to collect FISMA-related training information. However, a manager within the Office of the CIO at Commerce stated that the information collected by Commerce's system may not be entirely comprehensive, and Treasury officials reported that there were still certain manual data-gathering steps that fed into the automated system.

The large variation in the numbers reported to OMB, OPM, and us demonstrates the difficulties that agencies face in accurately tracking their cybersecurity workforce. It also illustrates the difficulties in relying on these numbers for workforce planning activities. However, developing a means to track the cybersecurity workforce will require a governmentwide effort to improve personnel systems. Until these improvements are made, agencies will continue to have difficulty gathering accurate data on the existing size of their cybersecurity workforce and making data-driven decisions for cybersecurity workforce planning.

Agencies Have Taken Steps to Define Cybersecurity Roles and Responsibilities and Related Skills and Competencies, but Lack Clear Guidance

We have previously reported that agencies should develop and adopt clearly defined roles and responsibilities and related skills and competencies to help ensure that personnel have the appropriate workload, skills, and training to perform their jobs effectively. In addition, we have stated that federal agencies that ensure they have high- performing employees with the appropriate skills and competencies are better able to meet their mission and goals.[19]

Several federal organizations have provided guidelines and tools for agencies to define cybersecurity roles and responsibilities. Specifically,

- The CIO Council has developed the following 11 cybersecurity roles, most recently updated in October 2010, that agencies can use as guidelines in developing detailed position descriptions and training.[20]
  - chief information officer
  - chief information security officer
  - digital forensics and incident response analyst
  - information security assessor
  - information security risk analyst
  - information systems security officer
  - information security systems and software development specialist
  - network security specialist
  - security architect
  - systems operations and maintenance professional
  - vulnerability analyst.

- NIST has described roles and responsibilities in Special Publication 800-37. This publication describes the roles and responsibilities of the key participants involved in an organization's risk management process including, among others, the chief information officer, information owner, senior information security officer, information system owner, information system security officer, and information security architect.[21] Additional NIST publications also define other cybersecurity roles and responsibilities.

- OPM developed a competency model for cybersecurity, released in February 2011, that lists key competencies for the cybersecurity workforce. OPM, in collaboration with an interagency working group, has also developed three broad categories for cybersecurity work: IT infrastructure, operations, maintenance, and information assurance; domestic law enforcement and counterintelligence; and specialized, and largely classified, cybersecurity operations focused on collection, exploitation, and response.

Federal agencies we reviewed had generally taken steps to fully or partially define cybersecurity roles and responsibilities and related skills and competencies based in part on these guidelines. For example,
- Commerce had defined operational roles, responsibilities, skills, and competencies for multiple cybersecurity roles based on Special Publication 800-37. The agency also defined skills and competencies through its training policy. For example, for the information system owner role, Commerce identified training and certifications that support the defined role based on competencies that the department identified.
- DOD had performed extensive work to outline roles, responsibilities, skills, and competencies in its cybersecurity workforce. DOD Directive 8570.01-M[22] defines the roles, responsibilities, competencies, and skills that DOD expects its cybersecurity workforce to possess. For example, the role of information assurance management level 1 is defined as having responsibility for the implementation and operation of a DOD information system. Additionally, the directive outlines skills such as user validation and competencies such as information assurance that are critical to the job.
- HHS has developed definitions of cybersecurity roles and responsibilities and has developed partial definitions of skills and competencies at the agency level for these positions. The HHS Information Systems Security and Privacy policy defines 31 roles and their corresponding responsibilities for the agency's cybersecurity program based, in part, on NIST guidelines. According to agency officials, HHS uses shared position descriptions to document certain skills and competencies through the job analysis process but has not undertaken efforts to fully define skills and competencies for cybersecurity positions.

- DHS has issued guidance that defines roles, responsibilities, skills, and competencies for its cybersecurity workforce based on both CIO Council and NIST guidelines. However, according to agency officials, use of the guidance is not consistent across all components of the agency.
- Justice has only partially defined roles and responsibilities and skills and competencies. Specifically, while selected individual components have developed detailed definitions for roles, responsibilities, skills, and competencies, the agency has not developed an overarching definition for the entire agency. According to the agency, this is due, in part, to the specialized nature of the work performed by Justice components.
- DOT has defined roles and responsibilities and skills and competencies for cybersecurity staff based in part on NIST guidelines in its cybersecurity strategic plan; however, the department stated it does not have time frames for implementing its strategic plan because of limited funding.
- Treasury has partially defined roles, responsibilities, skills, and competencies for the agency. Treasury has departmentwide policy defining roles and responsibilities for the cybersecurity workforce, but officials reported that because of the department's decentralized nature, they do not manage how roles and responsibilities are defined at the bureau level. Furthermore, Treasury officials stated that they only define skills and competencies in specific position descriptions, although this is, to some extent, based on OPM's competency model.
- VA has partially defined roles, responsibilities, skills, and competencies for the agency based on CIO Council and OPM guidelines. For the information security officer role, VA has defined a model that includes an extensive training program that addresses roles and responsibilities and needed skills and competencies. However, VA has not yet defined roles, responsibilities, skills, and com-petencies for the cybersecurity workforce except for the information security officer role. According to VA officials, the agency is planning on extending this model to other positions in the cybersecurity workforce but does not yet have estimated completion dates.

The approaches taken by each agency to define cybersecurity roles, responsibilities, skills, and competencies vary considerably. Some of these differences can be attributed to differences in mission, goals, and organization.

For example, officials within components of Justice—the Federal Bureau of Investigation (FBI) and Computer Crime and Intellectual Property Section—stated that certain aspects of their work did not fit into governmentwide cybersecurity definitions. Treasury officials also stated that because of the decentralized structure of their department, it would be difficult to centralize definitions of roles and responsibilities.

However, many of the differences can be attributed to the multiple sources of governmentwide guidance and their lack of alignment. The agencies we reviewed reported drawing on, to varying extent, the CIO Council definitions, NIST publications, and the OPM competency model. However, these three models all take different approaches to defining the cybersecurity workforce. For example, the matrices supporting the CIO Council's effort use roles, performance level, competencies, skills, suggested credentials, and suggested training. NIST Special Publication 800-37 describes roles and responsibilities for cybersecurity based on FISMA-related responsibilities. OPM's competency model addresses cybersecurity professionals in terms of series, grade, and competencies. There are enough differences in these sources of guidance to cause confusion for agencies. For example, the CIO Council matrices define a chief information security officer role, which, according to the CIO Council project lead, maps to the NIST senior information security officer role. However, the NIST framework also defines other roles, such as information owner and authorizing official, that do not map to roles defined by the CIO Council. While both organizations define an information security assessor role, the CIO Council defines this role as being autonomous from the organization, while NIST states that the level of independence of the assessor varies based on the specific conditions of the role. Until these multiple governmentwide efforts are more clearly aligned, agencies may have difficulty consistently defining these areas for themselves and avoiding duplication of effort.

Agencies Report Challenges in Filling Cybersecurity Positions

A high-performance organization needs a workforce with talent, multidisciplinary knowledge, and up-to-date skills in order to achieve its mission.[23] To recruit such a workforce for cybersecurity, agencies should develop recruiting and hiring efforts that are tailored to address gaps in the number, skills, and competencies of their cybersecurity workforce.

Table 4. Summary of Agency Reported Status of Efforts to Fill Cybersecurity Positions

Agency	Reported status
Commerce	Generally is able to find sufficient applicants to fill positions but sometimes has difficulty finding candidates with a combination of federal experience, detailed IT security knowledge, and professional certifications.
DOD	Reported difficulties with recruiting qualified cybersecurity staff. Identified barriers include processing time for security clearances, difficulty finding qualified candidates, and the hiring process. Additionally, the National Security Agency (NSA) has expressed concern that the future pipeline of talent may not be able to meet the agency's needs.
HHS	Generally able to fill open positions, but reports difficulty meeting current cybersecurity responsibilities with the current level of staffing. The department's Chief Information Security Officer cited continuing findings in the HHS Inspector General's evaluations and audits of the agency's implementation of FISMA as evidence of a lack of sufficient head count.
DHS	Reported being able to find qualified cybersecurity staff to fill positions generally, but a component—the National Cyber Security Division—has had trouble finding personnel for certain specialized areas, such as watch officers.
Justice	Officials from both Justice's Computer Crime and Intellectual Property Section and its CIO organization stated that a current hiring freeze limits their ability to determine if recruiting is a challenge. Officials from both the CIO organization and FBI stated that entry-level cybersecurity positions have generally been easier to fill than positions requiring more advanced technical knowledge.
DOT	The department stated that a lack of funding has prevented DOT from hiring personnel to fill cybersecurity positions recently.
Treasury	Treasury stated that there can be difficulty filling more technical cybersecurity positions, such as those dealing with penetration testing and forensic analysis, but there is not a consensus across the organization that finding qualified staff is a problem.
VA	VA officials stated that they are able to find qualified staff but have difficulty retaining them once they are trained, as they leave for higher-paying federal or contractor positions.

Source: GAO summary of agency written responses and interviews.

They should establish an active recruiting program with involvement from senior leaders and line managers and make use of strategies such as outreach to colleges and universities and internships.[24] In addition, administrative processes needed to hire a candidate should be streamlined to expedite hiring. An effective hiring process meets the needs of agencies and managers by filling positions with quality employees through the use of a timely, efficient, and transparent process.

Agencies' Ability to Fill Cybersecurity Positions Mixed

The agencies we reviewed varied in their ability to fill cybersecurity positions. (See table 4.) Specifically, officials at four of the eight agencies we reviewed stated that they were generally able to recruit and hire to fill needed cybersecurity positions. Officials at several agencies reported challenges in filling more technical positions, and officials at two agencies reported currently being under a hiring freeze.

In contrast to the other agencies we reviewed, only DOD provided specific numerical evidence of a shortage of cybersecurity personnel. DOD reported that for 2010, the department had more than 97,000 information assurance positions, but about 9,000 of these positions were unfilled. DOD's Cyber Command projected that as of September 2011, it would have more than 80 percent of available cyber positions filled. According to the department, its current vacancy level is due, in part, to Cyber Command being a relatively new organization, having been created in May 2010.

Officials at several agencies identified concerns with the availability of candidates for certain highly technical positions, such as network security engineers, malware analysts, and computer forensics experts. Specifically, Treasury and HHS officials stated that while they generally do not have problems filling cybersecurity positions, highly technical positions can be difficult to fill. Treasury officials stated that they use contractors to fill in the gaps for the hard-to-fill cybersecurity positions. Officials also identified challenges due to competition with both the private sector and other federal agencies that are able to offer more compensation for similar positions. In addition, officials at Commerce and DHS stated that they have not experienced difficulty in finding qualified cybersecurity staff for most positions, but have at times had trouble finding personnel who have the specialized skills they require.

Agencies Report Challenges with Administrative Processes, Including Hiring and Obtaining Security Clearances

Officials at the agencies we reviewed identified challenges with administrative processes for recruiting and hiring cybersecurity staff, including the length and complexity of the federal hiring process and delays in obtaining security clearances.

Specifically, officials at six of the eight agencies we reviewed identified the hiring process as an obstacle to hiring cybersecurity personnel. We have previously reported[25] and the administration has acknowledged[26] that the complexity and inefficiency of the federal hiring process has deterred many highly-qualified individuals from seeking and obtaining jobs. In order to recruit highly-qualified individuals such as those in security, some agencies stated they have used several different hiring authorities to help them recruit cybersecurity personnel; however, there was little documented evidence that suggested one particular hiring authority was more advantageous than another.[27] For example, some agencies use the direct hire authority or the excepted hire authority to recruit cybersecurity personnel, but they did not provide data on whether the different hiring authorities allowed them to hire more or better qualified cybersecurity professionals, or whether the hiring authority allowed them to bring the candidates aboard more quickly.

In May 2010, President Obama instructed federal executive agencies to streamline and improve the federal hiring process.[28] These changes included reducing the time it takes to hire new employees to less than 80 days, eliminating essay-style questions from initial job applications in favor of résumés and cover letters, adopting a category rating system[29] to provide managers with a larger applicant pool from which to select candidates, and requiring hiring managers and supervisors to be more involved in the hiring process. All of these changes were to have been implemented by November 2010. Agencies were to report on their progress in implementing the hiring reforms to OPM.

All eight of the agencies we reviewed reported having begun implementing the reforms, with almost all agencies reporting continuing efforts to improve the hiring process. DOD officials cautioned that it would take time for the full effect of the reforms to spread across the department. And some agencies, such as Justice, noted that because of a hiring freeze, they had not hired new cybersecurity staff, making the effectiveness of the reforms difficult to judge. Table 5 summarizes agency adoption of the hiring reforms.

Obtaining a security clearance for new employees was also identified by several officials as a challenge. For example, DOD's Cyber Command reported that it can take about a year to start a new employee because of both the lengthy hiring process and the time required to obtain a security clearance.

Table 5. Agency-Reported Implementation of the President's May 2010 Hiring Reforms

	Status of reform implementation
Commerce	Commerce's average time-to-hire in the third quarter of fiscal year 2011 was 75 days. Commerce officials reported the department had eliminated application essay questions in favor of résumés and implemented category rating for all of its hiring. Commerce did not provide data on improving manager involvement in the hiring process.
DOD	DOD's average time-to-hire in the third quarter of fiscal year 2011 was 70 days. DOD officials reported that work is ongoing to improve manager satisfaction with the quality of candidates and applicant satisfaction.
HHS	HHS's average time-to-hire in the third quarter of fiscal year 2011 was 52 business days. It has also implemented category rating departmentwide, and eliminated application essay questions in favor of résumés. HHS did not report on manager involvement in the hiring process because of low survey response rates.
DHS	DHS has eliminated application essay questions in favor of résumés, started to implement category ratings for all of its hiring, and reported training its managers and supervisors to be more involved in the hiring process, but did not report its average time-to-hire.
Justice	Justice officials reported that the department had implemented the hiring reforms, and indicated it has policies for the use of category rating, but provided no data on its elimination of application essay questions in favor of résumés, manager involvement in the hiring process, or its average time-to-hire.
DOT	DOT's average time-to-hire in the second quarter of fiscal year 2011 was 123 days. DOT officials reported implementing a category rating system, eliminating application essay questions in favor of résumés, taking steps to increase manager involvement in the hiring process.
Treasury	Treasury's average time-to-hire in the second quarter of fiscal year 2011 was 129 days. Treasury officials reported having implemented category rating departmentwide, and eliminated application essay questions in favor of résumés.
VA	VA reported an average time-to-hire of 95 days as of August 2011. The department also reported that it has eliminated application essay questions in favor of résumés, implemented category rating, and taken steps to increase managers' involvement in the hiring process.

Source: GAO summary of agency documentation.

We have previously reported on the challenges in timely adjudication of security clearance applications for federal employees and contractors, identifying delays in DOD's security clearance process as a high-risk area since 2005.[30] FBI reported continuing challenges with both obtaining initial clearances and processing clearances for cleared employees at other federal agencies that transfer to FBI. We recently reported that agencies had made substantial progress in reducing the time to obtain security clearances, and removed DOD's clearance process from our high-risk list in February 2011, but also reported that continuing work was needed in this area.[31]

Agency Use of Incentives to Recruit and Retain Cybersecurity Personnel Varies; Few Metrics Exist to Measure Their Effectiveness

Federal agencies have the authority to offer a variety of incentives to attract and retain personnel with the critical skills needed to accomplish their missions. These incentives can include recruitment, relocation, and retention incentive payments; student loan repayments; annual leave enhancements; scholarships; and student employment programs.

Each agency has the flexibility to determine which specific incentives of those authorized it chooses to offer.[32] If an agency offers recruitment, relocation, or retention incentives, it is required by regulation to track their implementation.[33] Furthermore, we have previously reported on the importance of establishing the necessary data and indicators to track an incentive program's effectiveness, as well as establishing a baseline to measure the changes over time and assess the program in the future.[34]

Several agencies and components of the agencies that we reviewed reported incentive programs that they have used for hiring and retaining cybersecurity personnel. (See table 6.)

Among the agencies we reviewed, DOD offered the broadest range of incentives to recruit and retain cybersecurity professionals. For example, DOD had scholarship programs, student employment programs, and recruitment incentives that can be offered to cybersecurity professionals or individuals who are studying to become cybersecurity professionals. In addition, DOD is seeking new authorities and incentives in order to improve its ability to recruit cybersecurity talent. These authorities range from expanded scholarships to retention incentives that are dependent on cybersecurity certifications.

Table 6. Reported Use of Incentives for Cybersecurity Workforce Recruiting and Retention at Selected Federal Agencies

Incentive	Commerce	DOD	HHS	DHS	Justice	DOT[a]	Treasury[b]	VA
Recruitment incentives	X	X			X	X		
Relocation incentives		X			X	X		
Retention incentives	X	X				X		
Superior qualifications and special needs pay-setting authority[c]	X	X			X	X		
Scholarships[d]		X						
Student employment programs	X	X				X		
Student loan repayments	X	X				X		
Annual leave enhancements		X			X	X		

Source: GAO analysis of agency documentation.

[a] DOT indicated it does not use scholarships or student loan repayments for cybersecurity recruiting at a department level, but the Federal Aviation Administration, a component of DOT, does make use of them.

[b] Treasury indicated that it does not make use of retention incentives or superior qualifications and special needs pay setting authority for cybersecurity employees, but the Internal Revenue Service, a component of Treasury, does make use of them.

[c] The superior qualifications and special needs pay setting authority allows an agency to set the rate of basic pay of an individual newly appointed to a General Schedule position at a rate above the minimum rate of the appropriate General Schedule grade based on the employee's superior qualifications or a special need of the agency.

[d] Refers to scholarships that are offered and funded by the agency we reviewed and does not count scholarships that are funded by an outside source such as the Scholarship for Service program.

At other agencies, incentives were less specifically focused on the cybersecurity workforce. Instead, agencies made targeted use of existing authorities and incentives in order to attract the individuals with the skills that they needed.

For example:

- DHS reported using incentives including recruitment and relocation incentives, superior qualifications and special needs pay setting authority, and annual leave enhancements, and plans to offer student loan repayments when negotiating with potential employees.
- Justice reported using incentives including recruiting, relocation, and retention incentives; superior qualifications and special needs pay setting authority; student employment programs; student loan repayments; and annual leave enhancements. Justice officials reported that use of these incentives is guided by departmental policy.
- Treasury components are permitted to use incentives, but have generally not found it necessary to employ them or do not have sufficient funds to use them. The Internal Revenue Service uses retention incentives and superior qualifications and special needs pay setting authority in lieu of other recruitment incentives.

Several agencies reported not using incentives, or using them sparingly. As noted, Treasury reported it had generally not found incentives to be necessary to recruit or retain cybersecurity workers. HHS reported that, given the state of the economy, it found it had large applicant pools to select from when hiring cybersecurity workers, making it unnecessary to use incentives. In addition, officials from FBI and the National Security Agency (NSA) told us that the unique missions of the organizations serve as a strong incentive for potential employees and compensate for lower salaries. Officials at VA said they were developing an incentive program.

Officials at several of the agencies we reviewed stated that they do not evaluate or have difficulty evaluating whether incentives effectively support hiring and retaining highly-skilled personnel in hard-to-fill positions. For example, DOD stated that the fact that its civilian incentive programs are neither centrally managed nor limited to selected occupational specialties makes it difficult to determine how effective the incentives are in retaining cybersecurity professionals. A Treasury official reported that because of the decentralized nature of the department and the difficulties in categorizing cybersecurity personnel, the department does not know the full extent of its use of incentives for cybersecurity recruiting and retention. Justice officials stated that, since incentive recipients must sign service agreements requiring them to work for the department for a set period of time, there is no need to perform any other kind of tracking.

Governmentwide evaluation of the effectiveness of incentives is also limited. During calendar years 2005 through 2009, Congress required OPM to produce annual governmentwide reports on the use of recruitment, relocation, and retention incentives at the series and grade levels. However, as previously discussed, cybersecurity responsibilities do not necessarily correspond to a specific job series. In August 2011, OPM reported that in calendar year 2009, federal agencies paid approximately $14.2 million in recruitment, relocation, and retention incentives to 1,269 IT workers in the 2210 occupation series, under which many, but not all, cybersecurity employees are classified.[35] In this report, OPM stated these incentives are important tools to help agencies attract and retain employees. However, OPM also stated its report is not intended to provide detailed information on the content or administration of agency incentive plans and policies, and that it does not verify the quality or accuracy of the agency-submitted data upon which it bases its report. Since the congressional mandate for this report has expired, OPM has issued proposed regulations that would continue the data gathering and reporting as an ongoing activity. In commenting on a draft of this report, OPM provided additional information on steps it was taking to improve oversight of incentives, including requesting updated baseline data on the use of incentives from agencies for calendar years 2010 and 2011, and setting limits on spending for incentives in calendar years 2011 and 2012.

We previously found that agencies had opportunities to improve oversight of their use of incentives,[36] and OPM has found that agencies' oversight of their incentives was not sufficient.[37] In February 2010, OPM outlined a plan to improve the oversight of the use of recruitment, relocation, and retention incentives governmentwide. As part of this plan, OPM has stated it would develop additional guidance and tools to assist agencies in the administration and oversight of their incentive programs, but has not yet done so. While the proposed regulations OPM issued would expand the scope of existing regulations by requiring agencies to review all retention incentives and recruitment incentives targeted at groups of employees at least annually to determine whether they should be revised or discontinued, these regulations have not been finalized.[38] Without finalized guidance from OPM, agencies will likely continue to face challenges in determining the effectiveness of their incentives in recruiting and retaining cybersecurity employees.

Differences in Compensation Systems Create Perception of Disparity in Agencies' Ability to Recruit and Retain Cybersecurity Professionals

A compensation system is a tool for attracting, motivating, retaining, and rewarding the people an agency needs to accomplish its mission and goals. Organizations examine their compensation systems to identify relevant constraints and flexibilities and make changes to support their human capital needs. Generally, the agencies we reviewed are subject to the General Schedule (GS) system of position classifications and grades to define positions and set salaries. In certain cases where agencies have had difficulty recruiting and retaining IT employees, OPM has authorized agencies to pay salaries higher than those under the regular GS system. We, the National Commission on the Public Service, and OPM have all called for the reform or replacement of the GS system and related performance management systems, citing factors including its inflexibility and its reliance on time in position rather than performance as a means of motivating and rewarding employees.[39]

Officials at two of the eight agencies we reviewed, as well as at OPM, said they believed the pay and flexibilities offered to applicants at agencies or agency components that do not use the GS system make those agencies more attractive to applicants, as compared with agencies that use the GS system. Officials at DHS and OPM identified NSA, and Treasury officials identified some of its own bureaus, such as the Office of the Comptroller of the Currency, as non-GS agencies that were more competitive when recruiting cybersecurity applicants, as they could offer higher salaries to cybersecurity employees than allowed under the GS system. However, as previously noted, DHS and Treasury stated that they are generally able to fill their cybersecurity positions.

For example, a flexibility in the compensation system NSA uses gives it a greater ability to pay employees more as they gain additional experience or responsibilities. The flexibility, called "rank-in-person," allows the agency to promote and pay an employee more as the employee gains additional experience or responsibilities without the employee needing to apply for a new position or requiring that a vacant position be available, as would be required under the GS system. In contrast, the GS system uses a "promotion-in-position" system, under which positions are classified at one or more grades (for example, GS-7, GS-9, GS-11, and GS-13). When an employee reaches the maximum salary permitted by the highest grade at which the position is classified, he or she must apply for a job classified at a higher grade to earn more. Furthermore, according to OPM, the salary at the highest step of a grade is only about 30 percent higher than the initial step, while alternative pay systems generally have considerably wider pay ranges. NSA officials stated that while they do not use the GS system's "promotion-in-position" system, NSA's hiring and personnel practices are more similar to those of the rest of the federal government than they are different. Table 7 summarizes some of the compensation flexibilities at non-GS-system components of agencies that we reviewed.

These differences in compensation systems among the agencies we reviewed have created the perception that agencies using non-GS compensation systems may have greater success in recruiting and retaining cybersecurity personnel. We have recently begun a review to examine previous recommendations to reform the federal pay systems. Identifying and implementing improvements to the GS pay and position classification systems may improve the government's ability to recruit and retain employees, including cybersecurity employees.

Table 7. Selected Compensation Flexibilities at Certain Non-GS-System Federal Agencies

Flexibility	Description
Pay banding	Salary ranges are set in 6-8 broad ranges (bands) rather than the 15 grades of the GS system.
Higher salaries	Agencies can offer higher salaries than at agencies that use the GS system.
Rank-in-person	Employee grade and pay levels are set based on the combination of qualifications and assignments, in addition to the responsibilities and duties of the position occupied.

Source: GAO analysis of agency data.

Training and Development Opportunities for Cybersecurity Workers Vary Widely among Agencies

Strategic human capital management centers on viewing people as assets whose value to an organization can be enhanced through investment in training and development activities to help employees build the competencies needed to achieve an agency's goals. We and OPM[40] have identified training programs and the earning of professional certifications as activities that support an employee's development of needed skills and competencies. As set forth in our guide, to ensure that agencies are making appropriate investments in training and development, agencies should also make fact-based determinations of the impact of their training and development programs.

Table 8 summarizes agency use of cybersecurity training programs and certification requirements.

Of the eight agencies we reviewed, three—Commerce, DOD, and VA—have departmentwide training programs for their cybersecurity workforce. Commerce and DOD also have certification requirements for cybersecurity positions. Specifically,

- In September 2010, Commerce established minimum training requirements for individuals in designated cybersecurity roles, and requires personnel in selected positions to hold relevant professional certifications. Commerce's Office of the CIO did not provide data on the number of individuals covered by this policy, although one official reported that in 2011, 40 employees were participating in its Cybersecurity Development Program, which prepares participants for certification.
- DOD's Information Assurance Workforce Improvement Program sets training and certification requirements for all agency personnel who perform information assurance functions, regardless of whether information assurance is an employee's primary duty. The program covered approximately 88,000 people as of calendar year 2010. Between fiscal years 2007 and 2011, DOD allocated more than $53 million to cover the cost of certifications and certification membership fees for the program, not including additional funds DOD components may have expended to support the program's execution. DOD officials said they found the certification requirement valuable based on feedback from DOD components. As an example of the benefits of the program, the department reported reductions in the number of identified vulnerabilities at a military command as the number of trained and certified employees increased. DOD further noted that it found the requirement for certificate owners to participate in continuing education to be valuable for keeping the skills of its cybersecurity workforce up-to-date. In addition, NSA and other DOD components have their own specialized training programs for cybersecurity personnel, with requirements above and beyond those of DOD's Information Assurance Workforce Improvement Program.

Table 8. Agency Cybersecurity Training and Development Programs and Practices

Agency	Training program	Certification requirement
Commerce	X	X
DOD	X	X
HHS		
DHS		
Justice[a]		
DOT		
Treasury		
VA	X	

Source: GAO analysis of agency documentation and interviews.

[a] Although Justice does not have an agencywide training program, FBI has a training program for its special agent personnel, including those working in cybersecurity.

- VA has a departmentwide training program that requires its information security officers to complete a 2-year training and mentoring program based on an internally-developed curriculum, which officials said resembles that of a private-sector professional certification. Participants are encouraged, but not required, to take the certification exam.

The remaining agencies do not have specific departmentwide cybersecurity training programs:

- The HHS Chief Information Security Officer reported that the agency budgets approximately $1,500 per cybersecurity employee for training and development activities and tailors individual development and training plans to employee needs, but does not have a structured training and development program for cybersecurity personnel.
- DHS officials reported that while it budgets $2,000 per person per year for training, the department does not have a specific training and development program for its cybersecurity personnel, though it is in the process of developing one.
- Justice officials said that while the department does not have a structured program for training cybersecurity personnel, it tailors employee individual development plans to meet the agency's needs. FBI, however, has a componentwide program providing specialized

cybersecurity training tailored to its agents' skills in accordance with the component's missions and goals. In addition, Justice officials stated that while the training required to earn a certification may be valuable, the certification requirement itself was of limited additional value, and thus did not require certification for employees.
- DOT does not currently have a departmentwide training program for its cybersecurity staff, although it reported that some components have such programs. The department stated that its cybersecurity strategic plan calls for the department to create an agencywide program, but that limited funding has affected this goal.
- Treasury officials reported that its components are responsible for developing their own cybersecurity training programs, based on their own unique needs. Treasury's Chief Information Security Officer also said that in his opinion, commercial certifications were often too general to be applied to specific cybersecurity positions.

MULTIPLE GOVERNMENTWIDE EFFORTS UNDER WAY TO ENHANCE CYBERSECURITY WORKFORCE, BUT EFFORTS LACK PLANNING AND COORDINATION

The federal government has begun several initiatives to enhance the federal cybersecurity workforce.

- The National Initiative for Cybersecurity Education (NICE) is an interagency effort coordinated by NIST to improve the nation's cybersecurity education, including efforts directed at the federal workforce. NIST has recently released a draft strategic plan for NICE for public comment, but the initiative lacks key details on activities to be accomplished and does not have clear authority to accomplish its goals.
- The CIO Council, N IST, OPM, and DHS all have separate efforts to develop a framework and models outlining cybersecurity roles, responsibilities, skills, and competencies. Officials reported plans to coordinate these efforts, but did not have specific time frames for doing so.
- The Information Systems Security Line of Business is a governmentwide initiative to create security training shared service centers. The effort is led by DHS and administered by DOD, the

National Aeronautics and Space Administration (NASA), State, and VA. Each center offers cybersecurity training for use by other agencies, but there are currently no plans to coordinate the centers' offerings or gather feedback on the training or incorporate lessons learned into revisions of the training.
- The IT Workforce Capability Assessment, administered by the CIO Council, is an effort to gather data on governmentwide IT training including cybersecurity. The assessment to occur every 2 years, CIO Council has no specific plans to use results of the assessments.
- DHS and NSF's Scholarship for Service program provides funding for undergraduate and graduate cybersecurity education in exchange for a commitment by recipients to work for the federal government. Most agencies we reviewed stated they believed the program was valuable. However, NSF currently does not track the longer-term value of the program by, for example, determining how many participants remain in government beyond their service commitment, but is working in an effort to develop and implement better ways to track this information.

NICE Has Recently Released a Draft Strategic Plan, but Lacks Governance Structure and Key Details on Achieving Goals

NICE began in March 2010 as an expansion of Initiative 8 of the Comprehensive National Cybersecurity Initiative, which focused on efforts to educate and improve the federal cybersecurity workforce.[41] According to the interagency committee recommendations establishing NICE, it is to provide program management support and promote intergovernmental efforts to improve cybersecurity awareness, education, workforce structure, and training. According to officials coordinating NICE activities, the efforts accomplished as part of the initiative include incorporating the Federal Information Systems Security Educators' Association[42] into NICE, launching the pilot of a virtual training environment for federal cybersecurity education, and releasing OPM's cybersecurity competency model.

In August 2011, NIST released a draft strategic plan for NICE, which provides high-level goals and a mission and vision. (See table 9.) Specifically, the plan states that the mission is to enhance the overall cybersecurity posture of the United States by accelerating the availability of educational and training resources designed to improve the cyber behavior, skills, and knowledge of every segment of the population.

Table 9. Goals of NICE

Goal	Participants	Description
1. Raise awareness about risks of online activities	DOD, DHS, Department of Education, NIST, NSF	A national cybersecurity awareness campaign intended to raise public awareness about the risks of online activities at home, in the workplace, and in communities.
2. Broaden the pool of skilled workers capable of supporting a cyber-secure nation	DHS, Department of Education, NIST, NSF, NSA	A set of programs intended to strengthen the pipeline of federal and private sector workers by bolstering formal cybersecurity education programs in kindergarten through 12th grade, with a focus on science, technology, engineering, and mathematics education.
3. Develop and maintain an unrivaled, globally competitive cybersecurity workforce	DOD, DHS, Department of Education, NIST, NSF, NSA, OPM	A series of efforts directed at workforce planning, professional development, and the identification of core professional competencies for the cybersecurity workforce, including the federal cybersecurity workforce. These efforts are directed at identifying and documenting skills, competencies, and the training necessary for the cybersecurity workforce to be effective.

Source: GAO analysis of NIST documentation.

While the NICE strategic plan describes several ambitious outcomes, the departments involved in NICE have not developed details on how they are going to achieve the outcomes. For example, the plan states that cybersecurity training will be aligned and integrated at all levels, federal agencies' human resources guidance should address cybersecurity work by 2013, and the workplace will see a 20-percent increase in qualified cybersecurity professionals by 2015. However, neither NICE nor participating agencies have released supporting plans to achieve these outcomes, such as current baseline information, needed resources, subtasks, and intermediate milestones.

Specific tasks under and responsibilities for NICE activities are also unclear. For example, the NICE strategic plan mentions the three goals listed in the previous table. Other NICE documentation refers to four components, each led by multiple agencies, that are similar to the goals. Furthermore, no comprehensive list of specific agency initiatives that are considered part of NICE has been published, and while NIST officials stated that each outcome listed in the strategic plan is based on input from a particular federal agency, the agency is not listed in the strategic plan, making it difficult to determine responsibility for the outcome.

Furthermore, NICE lacks a clear governance structure. According to NIST officials involved in NICE, specific initiatives under NICE are the responsibility of individual agencies, and those agencies will need to develop more detailed implementation plans. However, no time frame was provided for these plans to be developed. According to NIST officials coordinating NICE activities, NICE is primarily a consensus-driven group without a formal governance structure, and does not have authority to create or enforce goals or targets for individual agency activities. The officials also stated that the draft strategic plan would be revised based on public comments, but did not provide a deadline for its release.

Results-oriented strategic planning provides organizations with a set of performance goals for which they will be held accountable, measures progress toward those goals, determines strategies and resources to effectively accomplish the goals, uses performance information to make the programmatic decisions necessary to improve performance, and formally communicates the results in performance reports.

The lack of a clear governance structure and finalized and detailed plans means that the ability of NICE to achieve any of its goals, including those directed at the federal workforce, may be limited. Since NICE is an interagency working group with limited authority over its component organizations, clear governance, goals, milestones, and assignment of resources could help to ensure that the initiative performs as intended.

The CIO Council, NIST, OPM, and DHS Have All Taken Steps to Define Cybersecurity Roles and Competencies

To assist agencies, the CIO Council, NIST, OPM, and DHS have all engaged in separate efforts intended to help agencies define roles, responsibilities, skills, and competencies for their cybersecurity workforce.

CIO Council Is Developing Matrices to Identify Needed Cybersecurity Skills and Knowledge

In October 2010, the CIO Council released an updated version of 11 standard cybersecurity roles that agencies could use as a guideline in developing detailed position descriptions and training. (See table 10.)

Table 10. Information Security Roles as defined by the CIO Council

Role	Definition
Chief information officer	Focuses on information security strategy within an organization and is responsible for the strategic use and management of information, information systems, and IT.
Chief information security officer	Establishes, implements, and monitors the development and subsequent enforcement of the organization's information security program.
Digital forensics and incident response analyst	Performs a variety of highly technical analyses and procedures dealing with the collection, processing, preservation, analysis, and presentation of computer-related evidence, and is responsible for disseminating and reporting cyber-related activities, conducting vulnerability analyses, and risk management of computer systems and all applications during all phases of the system development life cycle.
Information security assessor	Oversees, participates in evaluating, and supports compliance issues pertinent to the organization.
Information security risk analyst	Facilitates and develops data-gathering methods to control and minimize risks by understanding external threats and vulnerabilities to the operation and environment.
Information systems security officer	Specializes in the information and security strategy within a system and is engaged throughout the systems development life cycle.
Information security systems and software development specialist	Securely designs, develops, tests, integrates, implements, maintains, or documents software applications (Web-based and non-Web), following formal secure systems development life cycle processes and using security engineering principles.
Network security specialist	Examines malicious software, suspicious network activities, and nonauthorized presence in the network to analyze the nature of a threat, and to secure and monitor firewall configurations.
Security architect	Implements business needs. Supports the business function as well as technology and environmental conditions (e.g., law and regulation), and translates them into security
	designs that support the organization to efficiently carry out its activities while minimizing risks from security threats and vulnerabilities.
Systems operations and maintenance professional	Supports and implements the security of information and information systems during the operations, maintenance, and enhancements phases of the systems development life cycle.
Vulnerability analyst	Detects threats and vulnerabilities in target systems, networks, and applications by conducting systems, network, and Web penetration testing.

Source: GAO analysis of CIO Council matrices.

For each role, the CIO Council plans to develop a workforce development matrix that lists suggestions for

- qualifications for entry, intermediate, and advanced performance levels for the role;
- additional sources for skill and competency materials;
- educational and professional credentials; and
- learning and development sources.

As of August 2011, the council had developed detailed matrices for four roles: chief information security officer, information security assessor, information security systems and software development professional, and systems operations and maintenance professional, and had drafted two additional matrices, for information systems security professional and information security auditor, which have not yet been released.

NIST Guidelines Outline Cybersecurity Responsibilities Related to FISMA

As part of its responsibilities under FISMA, NIST has defined cybersecurity roles and responsibilities in the following publications:[43]

- Special Publication 800-16, Information Security Training Requirements: A Role-and Performance-Based Model (draft);
- Special Publication 800-37, Guide for Applying the Risk Management Framework to Federal Information Systems; and
- Special Publication 800-50, Building an Information Technology Security Awareness and Training Program.

Table 11 identifies the cybersecurity roles defined in each publication.

As previously discussed, some of the roles in the NIST guidance map to roles the CIO Council has defined, while others do not. As of August 2011, NIST did not indicate plans to align the roles identified in NIST publications with the CIO Council roles. According to the agency, the roles are based on NIST's responsibilities under FISMA, and as such, do not need to be revised to align with the CIO Council roles. However, providing multiple unaligned sources of guidance to federal agencies limits the value of the guidance as a tool for agencies to use.

Table 11. Information Security Roles as defined by NIST Special Publications

Role	Definition	800-16	800-37	800-50
Head of agency (chief executive officer)	The highest-level senior official or executive within an organization with the overall responsibility to provide information security protect commensurate with the risk and magnitude of harm (i.e., impact) to organizational operations and assets, individuals, other organizations.	X	X	X
Chief information officer	Performs a variety of duties including developing and maintaining information security policies, procedures, and control techniques to address all applicable requirements; overseeing personnel with significant responsibilities for information security and ensuring that the personnel are adequately trained; assisting senior organizational officials concerning their security responsibilities; and coordinating with other senior officials.	X	X	X
Risk executive	Helps to ensure that risk-related considerations for individual information systems, to include authorization decisions, are viewed from an organizationwide perspective with regard to the overall strategic goals and objectives of the organization in carrying out its core missions and business functions and that information system-related security risks are consistent across the organization.		X	
Information owner/ steward	Responsible for establishing the policies and procedures governing the generation, collection, processing, dissemination, and disposal of information.		X	
Senior information security officer	Carries out the chief information officer security responsibilities under FISMA and serves as the primary liaison for the chief information officer to the organization's authorizing officials, information system owners, common control providers, and information system security officers.		X	
Senior agency information security officer	Responsible for the organization's information security awareness and training program.	X		

Role	Definition	800-16	800-37	800-50
Authorizing official	Senior official or executive with the authority to formally assume responsibility for operating an information system at an acceptable level of risk to organizational operations and assets, individuals, other organizations, and the nation.		X	
Authorizing official designated representative	An organizational official that acts on behalf of an authorizing official to coordinate and conduct the required day-to-day activities associated with the security authorization process.		X	
Common control provider	Responsible for the development, implementation, assessment, and monitoring of common controls.		X	
Information system owner	Responsible for the procurement, development, integration, modify-cation, operation, maintenance, and disposal of an information system.		X	
Information system security officer	Ensures that the appropriate operational security posture is maintained for an information system and as such, works in close collaboration with the information system owner.		X	
Information security architect	Ensures that the information security requirements necessary to protect the organization's core missions and business processes are adequately addressed in all aspects of enterprise architecture including reference models, segment and solution architectures, and the resulting information systems supporting those missions and business processes.		X	
Information system security engineer	Captures and refines information security requirements and ensures that the requirements are effectively integrated into IT component products and information systems through security architecture, design, development, and configuration.		X	
Security control assessor	Conducts a comprehensive assessment of the management, operational, and technical security controls employed within or inherited by an information system to determine the overall effectiveness of the controls.		X	
IT security program manager	Responsible for the information security awareness and training program.			X

Table 11. (Continued)

Role	Definition	800-16	800-37	800-50
Managers	Responsible for complying with information security awareness, awareness training, and role-based training requirements established for their employees, users, and those who have been identified as having significant responsibilities for information security.	X		X
Instructional design specialists	Develops information security awareness training and role-based courses.	X		
Personnel with significant responsibili-ties for information security	Personnel who should understand that information security is an integral part of their job; what the organization expects of them; how to implement and maintain information security controls; mitigate risk to information and information systems; monitor the security condition of the security program, system, application, or information for which they are responsible; or what to do when security breaches are discovered.	X		
Users	Largest audience in any organization and the single most important group of people who can help reduce unintentional errors and related information system vulnerabilities.	X		X

Source: GAO summary of NIST publications.

OPM Has Developed a Competency Model for Cybersecurity, but Has No Plans to Track Use or Revise

In 2009, OPM, in coordination with the CIO Council and a subcommittee of the Chief Human Capital Officers Council, identified cybersecurity as a high priority for developing a governmentwide cybersecurity competency model. As a part of this effort, OPM convened a series of focus groups to help develop a survey that was distributed in 2010 to cybersecurity professionals across the federal government. The survey, which was released in February 2011, was used to develop a competency model for the four most common job series used by cybersecurity professionals.[44]

The five competencies that were identified by the model as most important for cybersecurity professionals are listed in table 12.

Table 12. Top Five Competencies Identified by OPM's Cybersecurity Competency Model

Competency	Description
Integrity/ honesty	Contributes to maintaining the integrity of the organization; displays high standards of ethical conduct and understands the impact of violating these standards on an organization, self, and others; is trustworthy.
Computer skills	Uses computers, software applications, databases, and automated systems to accomplish work.
Technical competence	Uses knowledge that is acquired through formal training or extensive on-the-job experience to perform one's job; works with, understands, and evaluates technical information related to the job; advises others on technical issues.
Teamwork	Encourages and facilitates cooperation, pride, trust, and group identity; fosters commitment and team spirit; works with others to achieve goals.
Attention to detail	Is thorough when performing work and conscientious about attending to detail.

Source: OPM competency model.

Future adoption of the model may be limited for several reasons. First, the competency model is dominated by competencies that are not unique to cybersecurity. None of the top five competencies that are identified as important are specific to cybersecurity work. OPM officials stated that the "technical competence" competency could be further defined by an agency with specific cybersecurity skills for a particular position. Second, adoption of the cybersecurity workforce competency model is optional for agencies. OPM does not plan to track usage of the competency model by individual agencies, nor does it plan to collect feedback on the usefulness of the model or update it.

OPM officials stated that they believe the cybersecurity competency model will be adopted throughout the federal government. However, until OPM tracks usage of the competency model, collects feedback on the model, and develops plans to update it in response to feedback, the usefulness of the model may be unknown.

DHS Is Developing a Framework to Characterize the National Cybersecurity Workforce, with Future Plans to Align other Models and Frameworks

DHS is developing a framework supporting NICE that is intended to provide common language for describing the cybersecurity workforce.

The framework consists of 31 specialties, spread across seven categories of cyber-security work. The seven categories are listed in table 13.

For each specialty, DHS has developed a brief summary description of the specialty, a list of tasks performed by individuals in that specialty, and a list of knowledge, skills, and abilities someone in that specialty should have. The list maps to the technical competencies in OPM's cybersecurity competency model. A DHS official responsible for the framework stated that the draft framework was developed with input primarily from members of the intelligence community and DOD.

A draft of the framework was released for public comment in September 2011. DHS reports it is seeking input from academia, cybersecurity organizations, and the private sector as it continues to develop and refine the framework.

Table 13. DHS/NICE Cybersecurity Framework Work Categories

Category	Description
Securely provision	Conceptualizing, designing, and building secure IT systems, with responsibility for some aspect of the systems' development.
Operate and maintain	Providing the support, administration, and maintenance necessary to ensure effective and efficient IT system performance and security.
Protect and defend	Identification, analysis, and mitigation of threats to internal IT systems or networks.
Investigate	Investigation of cyber events/crimes of IT systems, networks, and/or digital evidence.
Operate and collect	Highly specialized and largely classified collection of cybersecurity information that may be used to develop intelligence.
Analyze	Highly specialized and largely classified review and evaluation of incoming cybersecurity information to determine its usefulness for intelligence.
Support	Providing support so that others may effectively conduct their cybersecurity work.

Source: NICE.

According to DHS's Director of National Cybersecurity Education Strategy, once the DHS/N ICE framework has been finalized, other federal documents, including NIST Special Publication 800-16 and the document governing DOD's Information Assurance Workforce Improvement Program, among others, will be rewritten to conform to it, but she did not provide a time frame for this to occur.

CIO Council, OPM, and DHS Report Plans to Coordinate Efforts, but Lack Specific Time Frames

While officials with the CIO Council, OPM, and DHS reported that steps are being taken to coordinate their various efforts related to defining the cybersecurity workforce, at the moment, each one, along with existing NIST guidelines, takes a different approach, using different categorizations of roles and terminology. The CIO Council's Workforce Development Matrices use roles, performance levels, competencies, skills, suggested credentials, and suggested training; NIST guidelines are based on FISMA-related responsibilities; OPM's competency model addresses cybersecurity professionals in terms of series, grade, and competencies; and the DHS/N ICE framework uses work categories, specialties, tasks, and knowledge, skills, and abilities. According to CIO Council representatives responsible for developing the matrices and NICE officials, the matrices, frameworks, and special publication were developed from different perspectives, but the officials acknowledged that in future versions they could be better aligned. Officials did not identify any specific time frames for these activities.

While NIST guidelines are already widely used throughout the federal government, there are currently no specific steps to promote the use of the other efforts' products governmentwide. OPM officials have stated that agency use of its competency model is voluntary, and representatives of the CIO Council and NICE have all stated they have no authority to require federal agencies to make use of their products, and did not identify specific steps they were taking to promote their use in the federal government. The DHS official responsible for development of the DHS/N ICE framework stated other relevant documents would be rewritten to conform to the framework, but the NICE lead at NIST stated that NICE can only build consensus, not mandate standards.

The CIO Council, NIST, OPM, and DHS/NICE efforts could help individual agencies in their own workforce planning efforts, reducing the amount of work each agency may have to do on its own. However, having multiple entities develop similar role and competency models is not an efficient use of resources. We have previously reported[45] that reducing or eliminating duplication in government programs could save billions of tax dollars annually and help agencies provide more efficient services. Until these organizations take steps to consolidate and better coordinate their efforts, it is unlikely that any of these efforts will be able to maximize its effectiveness, or that agencies will be able to reconcile their roles and responsibilities in an efficient and effective manner.

Information Systems Security Line of Business Has Multiple Providers for Cybersecurity Training, but Training Efforts Are Not Coordinated or Evaluated by DHS

In 2005, OMB and DHS collaborated on an initiative, called the Information Systems Security Line of Business, to address common information systems security needs across the government, including cyber-security training. DHS authorized five agencies to be security training shared service centers available to all federal agencies so as to reduce duplication and improve the quality of information security training. The training courses that they offer are organized into two training tiers: general security awareness training and role-based security training, which is offered by four of the five agencies, specifically State, DOD, NASA, and VA. The role-based security training is focused on individuals who perform significant cybersecurity tasks as part of their job. Agencies are required by FISMA to ensure that these individuals receive appropriate training for those tasks. The status of the training provided by each shared service center follows.

State/DOD

State is involved in a pilot effort, sponsored by DHS, to deliver online role-based cybersecurity training to up to 125,000 federal employees, called the Federal Virtual Training Environment (FedVTE). FedVTE includes content from DOD's role-based training. State reported that the environment currently holds about 800 hours of recorded classroom training and over 75 hands-on labs. The agency also stated that a phased rollout of FedVTE is planned to begin in the second quarter of fiscal year 2012 contingent on the successful completion of the pilot. A companion program, the Federal Cybersecurity Training Exercise (FedCTE), is also being developed. FedCTE supplements the online FedVTE training with in-person training.

NASA

NASA offers cybersecurity training for nine cybersecurity roles, such as system administrator and chief information officer, and makes the training available at no charge to other agencies on compact disc. This training was developed for use at NASA, and the role-based training courses were developed for NASA purposes. NASA officials stated that the training is customizable, but they do not provide support in customizing the courses for use by other federal agencies.

VA

VA has developed training for nine roles, and has made them available to other federal agencies through Web-based training. The courses cover topics such as fundamentals of cybersecurity, FISMA controls and reporting, and system certification and accreditation. VA officials stated that while they have an interest in customizing the training to support other agencies, they currently do not have a process in place to do so. For example, the agency does not have a means of accepting reimbursement for the costs of customization.

In order to build the capacity they need to achieve their missions and goals, federal agencies need to make wise decisions when investing in training and development programs for their workforce. We have previously reported[46] that agencies need to evaluate their training programs to ensure that they are successfully enhancing the skills and competencies of their employees and that reducing or eliminating duplication in government programs could save billions of tax dollars annually and help agencies provide more efficient services.[47]

While one of the goals of the shared program is to reduce duplication, there are several areas in which the training roles overlap among the agencies, and no process exists for coordinating or eliminating duplication among the efforts. For example, NASA, VA, and State all have training for employees in system administrator roles. Additionally, both NASA and VA offer training for CIOs, and NASA and State both offer training directed at the system owner role. As a result, an increased risk exists that training providers are offering duplicative training. DHS officials stated they are just starting to consider better coordination of the training centers, but did not have a specific plan for doing so. Reducing or eliminating duplication and overlap among the shared service providers would allow for more efficient and effective training to be offered by each agency, and could allow for a greater amount of training and broader range of courses to be provided at the same expense.

Additionally, DHS does not have, and does not require training providers to offer, a mechanism for gathering feedback on training and incorporating lessons learned into revisions, so there are no data available on how useful the current training is or means to compare the training of the different providers. DHS stated that it did not have authority to require training providers to gather feedback or incorporate lessons learned into the training provided. However, soliciting and acting on feedback could provide a means for the training offerings to be more effective and more broadly used.

CIO Council's IT Workforce Capability Assessment Revealed Governmentwide Cybersecurity Training Needs

The IT Workforce Capability Assessment is an effort by the CIO Council to gather data on the training needs of the federal IT workforce, including those who work in cybersecurity. The assessment, which stems in part from a requirement in the Clinger-Cohen Act that agencies assess the training needs of their IT staff, was originally intended to be an annual effort and was first conducted in 2003.[48] However, according to officials responsible for the effort, because of budget limitations, it was not conducted again until 2006 and then again in 2011.

The CIO Council stated that participating agencies are to use the agency-level data to support their workforce planning efforts and the aggregate data to provide an overall snapshot of the capabilities and skills of the federal IT workforce. In June, the CIO Council released the results of this year's assessment, which included for the first time a supplemental assessment of the cybersecurity workforce. Survey participants who indicated they perform cyberecurity activities were asked to rate their proficiency on the cybersecurity technical competencies identified in OPM's cybersecurity competency model and to identify competencies in which they and their organizations could benefit from training. About 42 percent of the approximately 18,000 survey respondents identified themselves as performing cybersecurity work. These participants rated their proficiency in the technical competencies identified in

OPM's cybersecurity competency model on a five-point scale, and also identified competencies in which they and their organizations needed additional training.

Training in forensics and vulnerabilities assessment topped the list of individual and organizational training needs, according to the survey results. Tables 14 and 15 detail the top five individual and organizational training needs, respectively.

While current plans are for the assessment to be conducted every 2 years, of the eight agencies we reviewed, only DOD and DHS identified specific plans to use the assessment data. Furthermore, the CIO Council does not have any specific plans for the use of the governmentwide survey data. We have previously identified surveys as a useful tool for gathering information on employee skills and training needs,[49] but unless this information is used to inform training and development efforts, the effort spent gathering it will likely be wasted. Accordingly, unless the assessment results are integrated into existing agency and governmentwide workforce planning and training activities, their value is limited.

Table 14. Top Five Individual Cybersecurity Competency Training Needs

Individual training need	Number of respondents	Percentage of total
Forensics	3,306	44.4
Computer network defense	3,193	42.9
Vulnerabilities assessment	2,952	39.6
Communications security management	2,093	28.1
Incident management	1,852	24.9

Source: CIO Council reported survey responses.

Table 15. Top Five Organizational Cybersecurity Competency Training Needs

Organizational training need	Number of respondents	Percentage of total
Vulnerabilities assessment	2,607	35.8
Computer network defense	2,407	32.3
Compliance	2,146	28.8
Communications security management	2,054	27.6
Incident management	1,920	25.8

Source: CIO Council reported survey responses.

Scholarship for Service Program Produces Skilled Cybersecurity Workers, but Long-Term Retention in Government Is Unknown

The Scholarship for Service (SFS) program, cosponsored by NSF and DHS, provides scholarships and stipends to undergraduate and graduate students who are pursuing information security-related degrees. In exchange for this financial support, the student must agree to work in an IT internship with the federal government while in school and to take a full-time cybersecurity position with the government after graduation for up to 2 years. In calendar years 2009 and 2010, the SFS program produced 203 graduates, of which approximately 95 percent had secured a cybersecurity position with the government as of December 2010. DOD and its components hired 49 percent of the program's graduates in that period, with 24 percent going to NSA, and the remaining 25 percent being hired by the military services and the civilian DOD. According to NSF, the program costs approximately $14 million per year.

Most of the agencies we talked with stated that the SFS program is a valuable resource for recruiting cybersecurity professionals; however, it is a relatively small program, graduating approximately 125 to 150 cybersecurity students each year. This number, when spread across 24 major federal agencies, does not provide a significant number of cybersecurity workers to meet the needs of the federal government.

It is also unclear how many of these students remain in federal service after their service repayment period has been fulfilled. An NSF official responsible for the program stated that it is difficult to track the retention rate of the students after their fulfillment is completed and that the agency has no accurate way of knowing how many students stay in the federal government. The official noted that the agency is currently working with two different groups in an effort to develop and implement better ways to track the students that are in repayment to determine whether they remain in federal work (including employment at intelligence agencies) after their contractual obligations have been completed. Until NSF develops and establishes effective tracking mechanisms to capture the retention rates of students beyond their contractual obligations, it is unclear how beneficial the program is in relation to other federal cybersecurity workforce development activities.

CONCLUSION

Federal agencies vary in their implementation of planning practices for their cybersecurity workforce. Five agencies have addressed several key principles in their workforce plans, but three agencies did not have any workforce plans that addressed cybersecurity needs. A challenge in cybersecurity workforce planning is the difficulty in defining and identifying cybersecurity workers. Further, many agencies have taken steps to define cybersecurity roles, responsibilities, skills, and competencies, but are hampered by the inconsistent alignment of existing governmentwide guidance. Agencies reported mixed results in filling cybersecurity positions, with specific challenges in filling highly technical positions and with hiring and security clearance processes, but are taking steps to address these challenges. Use of incentives for cybersecurity positions varied widely by agency, with DOD offering the widest range of incentives. However, no data exist on the effectiveness of incentives, in part because of the lack of guidance on tracking such data from OPM. Differences in compensation systems also affected agency perceptions of their ability to recruit cybersecurity personnel. Training and development opportunities also vary widely at agencies.

Several governmentwide efforts to improve cybersecurity workforce planning activities are under way, but NICE, which is intended to promote governmentwide cybersecurity efforts, lacks finalized and detailed plans needed to help ensure its goals are achieved. Multiple efforts by the CIO Council, NIST, OPM, and DHS have defined cybersecurity roles, responsibilities, skills, and competencies, but these efforts are potentially duplicative and could be better coordinated. Similarly, multiple efforts to assess and provide training needs are under way, but lack coordination. In an era of limited financial resources, better coordinated efforts to address both cybersecurity-specific and broader federal workforce challenges are crucial to cost-effectively ensuring that the government has the people it needs to continue to deal with evolving cyber threats.

RECOMMENDATIONS FOR EXECUTIVE ACTION

To improve individual agency cybersecurity workforce planning efforts, we are making the following recommendations:

- We recommend that the Secretary of Commerce direct the department's Chief Information Officer, in consultation with its Chief Human Capital Officer, to develop and implement a departmentwide cybersecurity workforce plan or ensure that departmental components are conducting appropriate workforce planning activities.
- We recommend that the Secretary of Defense direct the department's Chief Information Officer, in consultation with the Deputy Assistant Secretary for Defense for Civilian Personnel Policy, to update its departmentwide cybersecurity workforce plan or ensure that departmental components have plans that appropriately address human capital approaches, critical skills, competencies, and supporting requirements for its cybersecurity workforce strategies.
- We recommend that the Secretary of Health and Human Services direct the department's Chief Information Officer, in consultation with its Chief Human Capital Officer, to develop and implement a departmentwide cybersecurity workforce plan or ensure that departmental components are conducting appropriate workforce planning activities.
- We recommend that the Secretary of Transportation direct the department's Chief Information Officer, in consultation with its Chief Human Capital Officer, to update its departmentwide cybersecurity workforce plan or ensure that departmental components have plans that fully address gaps in human capital approaches and critical skills and competencies and supporting requirements for its cybersecurity workforce strategies.
- We recommend that the Secretary of Treasury direct the department's Chief Information Officer, in consultation with its Chief Human Capital Officer, to develop and implement a departmentwide cybersecurity workforce plan or ensure that departmental components are conducting appropriate workforce planning activities.
- We recommend that the Secretary of Veterans Affairs direct the department's Chief Information Officer, in consultation with its Chief Human Capital Officer, to update its departmentwide cybersecurity competency model or establish a cybersecurity workforce plan that fully addresses gaps in human capital approaches and critical skills and competencies, supporting requirements for its cybersecurity workforce strategies, and monitoring and evaluating agency progress.

To help federal agencies better identify their cybersecurity workforce, we recommend the Director of the Office of Personnel Management, in coordination with the Director of the Office of Management and Budget, collaborate with the CIO Council to identify and develop governmentwide strategies to address challenges federal agencies face in tracking their cybersecurity workforce.

To ensure that governmentwide cybersecurity workforce initiatives are better coordinated and planned, and to better assist federal agencies in defining roles, responsibilities, skills, and competencies for their workforce, we recommend that the Secretary of Commerce, Director of the Office of Management and Budget, Director of the Office of Personnel Management, and Secretary of Homeland Security collaborate through the NICE initiative to take the following three actions:

- clarify the governance structure for NICE to specify responsibilities and processes for planning and monitoring of initiative activities;
- develop and finalize detailed plans allowing agency accountability, measurement of progress, and determination of resources to accomplish agreed-upon activities; and
- consolidate and align efforts to define roles, responsibilities, skills, and competencies for the federal cybersecurity workforce.

To improve governmentwide cybersecurity workforce planning efforts, we recommend the Director of the Office of Personnel Management take the following actions:

- finalize and issue guidance to agencies on how to track the use and effectiveness of incentives for hard-to-fill positions, including cybersecurity positions and
- maximize the value of the cybersecurity competency model by (1) developing and implementing a method for ensuring that the competency model accurately reflects the skill set unique to the cybersecurity workforce, (2) developing a method for collecting and tracking data on the use of the competency model, and (3) creating a schedule for revising or updating the model as needed.

To improve governmentwide cybersecurity workforce planning efforts, we recommend that the Director of the Office of Management and Budget direct the CIO Council to develop a strategy for and track agencies' use of the IT Workforce Capability Assessment data.

To ensure that the benefits of the training provided through the Information Systems Security Line of Business are maximized, and resources are used most efficiently, we recommend the Secretary of the Department of Homeland Security take the following two actions:

- implement a process for tracking agency use of line of business training and gathering feedback from agencies on the training's value and opportunities for improvement and
- develop a process to coordinate training offered through the line of business to minimize the production and distribution of duplicative products.

To better determine the value to the government of the Scholarship for Service program, we recommend that the Director of the National Science Foundation develop and implement a mechanism to track the retention rate of program participants beyond their contractual obligation to the government.

AGENCY COMMENTS AND OUR EVALUATION

We provided a draft of this report to the agencies in our review. Of the six agencies to which we made individual recommendations regarding their workforce planning activities, five concurred and one agency neither concurred nor nonconcurred with our recommendations. A summary of comments follow.

- The Secretary of Commerce provided written comments in which the department generally concurred with our recommendation that it develop and implement a departmentwide cybersecurity workforce plan or ensure that departmental components are conducting appropriate workforce planning activities.
- The Acting Assistant Secretary of Defense for Networks and Information Integration/DOD CIO provided written comments in which the department concurred with our recommendation that it update its departmentwide cybersecurity workforce plan or ensure that departmental components have plans that appropriately address human capital approaches, critical skills, competencies, and

supporting requirements for cybersecurity workforce strategies. The draft version of this report contained an additional recommendation to DOD regarding the agency's certification program. Based on additional discussions with the department, we have deleted this recommendation.
- The Assistant Secretary for Legislation for the Department of Health and Human Services provided written comments in which the department concurred with our recommendation to develop and implement a departmentwide cybersecurity workforce plan or ensure that departmental components are conducting appropriate workforce planning activities and stated that the Office of the Chief Information Officer will coordinate with the Office of Human Resources to accomplish this with a target completion date of July 2012.
- The Deputy Director of Audit Relations for the Department of Transportation stated in oral comments that the department would not be providing formal written comments on our report and neither concurred nor nonconcurred with our recommendation to update its departmentwide cybersecurity workforce plan or ensure that departmental components have plans to address gaps in human capital approaches and critical skills and competencies and supporting requirements for its cybersecu rity workforce strategies.
- The Deputy Assistant Secretary for Information Systems and Chief Information Officer for the Department of the Treasury provided written comments in which the department concurred with our recommendation to develop and implement a departmentwide cyber-security workforce plan or ensure that departmental components are conducting appropriate workforce planning activities and stated that instructions will be issued to Treasury components requiring them to develop and submit plans to the department for evaluation and feedback.
- The Chief of Staff for the Department of Veterans Affairs provided written comments in which the department concurred with our recommendation to update its departmentwide cybersecurity competency model or establish a cybersecurity workforce plan that fully addresses gaps in human capital approaches and critical skills and competencies and supporting requirements for its cybersecurity workforce strategies, and stated that the Chief Information Officer and Chief Human Capital Officer will create and monitor an updated

departmentwide cybersecurity workforce plan that addresses all noted deficiencies in a phased approach with a target completion date of January 30, 2013.

Of the five agencies to which we made recommendations to address governmentwide challenges, four agencies—Commerce, DHS, OPM, and NSF—provided written comments on our recommendations. OMB did not provide written comments, but the OMB audit liaison did provide suggestions regarding the wording of our recommendations via e-mail, which we have considered. A summary of the responses from the four agencies follows.

- With respect to our recommendation to OMB and OPM to improve tracking of the federal cybersecurity workforce, the Associate Director of OPM Employee Services stated that the department concurred with our recommendation and that OPM will develop a data element for tracking the cybersecurity workforce in its Enterprise Human Resource Integration system and collaborate with the CIO Council, OMB, and other agencies as needed.
- With respect to our recommendation to Commerce, DHS, OMB, and OPM to clarify the governance structure and develop and finalize detailed plans for NICE, and to consolidate and align efforts to define roles, responsibilities, skills, and competencies for the federal cybersecurity workforce, agencies provided the following comments:
  - The Secretary of Commerce concurred with our recommendation and outlined steps NIST is taking with other NICE components to develop more detailed plans for NICE activities.
  - The Director of DHS's Departmental GAO-OIG Liaison Office concurred with our recommendation and stated that the department will coordinate with its NICE counterparts to document the existing governance structure, ensure a system for accountability, and define federal cybersecurity workforce roles, responsibilities, skills, and competencies. In oral comments, DHS officials stated the importance of NICE components agreeing to undertake specific activities before more detailed plans could be developed.
  - The Associate Director of OPM Employee Services partially concurred with our recommendation on governance structure and developing and finalizing detailed plans, stating that it does not have the authority to implement recommendations involving NICE governance structure, and should be removed from this part

of the recommendation. We acknowledge that NICE is a collaborative effort of multiple agencies. However, OPM does have key responsibilities for NICE, along with other federal agencies. As a result, we continue to address our recommendation regarding governance structure and plans to OPM together with Commerce, DHS, and OMB. We have clarified the wording of the recommendation to reflect our intent that this be a collaborative effort. The associate director concurred with our recommendation to consolidate and align efforts for federal cybersecurity workforce roles, responsibilities, skills and competencies.
- With respect to our recommendation to finalize and issue guidance to agencies on tracking the use and effectiveness of incentives, the Associate Director of OPM Employee Services stated that the department concurred with our recommendation and identified steps OPM is taking to address federal agencies' use of incentives.
- The Associate Director of OPM Employee Services did not concur with our draft recommendation to maximize the value of OPM's cybersecurity competency model by ensuring its accuracy, tracking its use, and revising it on a regular basis. She stated that the agency's methodology for developing the model was consistent with legal and professional guidelines, that use of the model is optional, and that OPM is working with OMB to reduce human capital reporting requirements, rather than establishing new requirements. However, during our review, OPM was unable to demonstrate the extent to which agencies were using the cybersecurity competency model. Given that none of the competencies identified by the model as being most important are specific to cybersecurity, following up with agencies to see if the model is actually used and if it needs revision is important. Thus, we believe that the components of our recommenddation to ensure the model accurately reflects the skill sets unique to the cybersecurity workforce and to track its use continue to have merit. The Associate Director also took exception with the component of our draft recommendation to create a schedule for revising or updating the model on a regular basis. She expressed concerns about the effort required for revising the model and indicated that models should be updated on an as-needed basis, rather than on an arbitrary timeline. We agree and have modified our recommendation accordingly.

- The Director of DHS's Departmental GAO-OIG Liaison Office concurred with our recommendations to DHS regarding improvements to the Information Systems Security Line of Business and stated that the department is developing a shared service center point of contact list for an annual data call for input toward future solutions to address our recommendation and will work with other shared service centers to ensure that they align with NICE activities and findings.
- The NSF Deputy Director concurred with our recommendation to develop a mechanism to track the retention rate of the Scholarship for Service program, but stated that our recommendation implied that the foundation was not planning to address this issue. The deputy director stated that the foundation is in the process of implementing a new monitoring and evaluation system to collect this type of data that will be operational in early 2012.

Several agencies also provided technical comments that were incorporated into our report as appropriate.

Gregory C. Wilshusen
Director,
Information Security Issues

Valerie C. Melvin
Director,
Information Management and Human Capital Issues

APPENDIX I. OBJECTIVES, SCOPE, AND METHODOLOGY

The objectives of our review were to assess (1) the extent to which key federal agencies have implemented established workforce planning practices for cybersecurity personnel and (2) the status of and plans for governmentwide cybersecurity workforce initiatives.

The scope of our effort for the first objective was limited to the eight largest federal agencies based on information technology (IT) spending: the Departments of Defense (DOD), Homeland Security (DHS), Health and Human Services (HHS), Treasury, Veterans Affairs (VA), Commerce, Transportation (DOT), and Justice. We determined IT spending by using the average of spending estimates that federal agencies provided to the Office of Management and Budget (OMB) from fiscal year 2009 through fiscal year 2011.

To determine the extent to which these key federal agencies had implemented principles of workforce planning in their workforce plans, we compared each of the five GAO key principles that strategic workforce planning should address with the agencies' workforce plans. If the agencies' workforce plans fully addressed all of the elements under each principle, we considered the agency to have fully addressed the principle. If the agency addressed at least two elements of the principle, we considered the agency to have partially addressed the principle. We did not review the department's efforts to implement the key principles discussed in the workforce plans.

To determine the ability of agencies to determine the number of cybersecurity staff at the agency, we gathered data from OMB's 2010 report on the Federal Information Security Management Act (FISMA), data the Office of Personnel Management (OPM) provided that it had collected from its data gathering efforts with agencies, individual agency FISMA reports, and information provided directly from agencies on their cybersecurity workforce. We compared the data from the different sources, reviewed the data for obvious outliers and errors, and verified them with agency officials. We used this information to illustrate the problems with reliably identifying cybersecurity employees and determined it was sufficient for this purpose.

To assess agency definitions of roles and responsibilities and skills and competencies for cybersecurity staff, we analyzed agency policies and documentation, supplemented with interviews with agency officials, to determine the extent to which the agency had developed definitions based on either National Institute of Standards and Technology (NIST) or federal Chief Information Officers (CIO) Council guidelines. We considered an agency to have partially developed roles and responsibilities or skills and competencies if it had either only developed selected definitions or had not implemented definitions across the entire agency.

To determine the extent to which agencies had implemented additional leading practices in workforce planning for cybersecurity personnel, we reviewed our own guidance and reports on federal agencies' workforce planning and human capital management efforts. We then analyzed agency documentation related to its cybersecurity workforce, including hiring and training plans, numbers of vacant and filled cybersecurity positions, use of recruitment and retention incentives, and information on salary structure and related personnel systems. We used this information to determine the extent of each agency's efforts to identify critical cybersecurity skills and competencies needed, challenges in developing or obtaining these skills and competencies, and plans to address these challenges based on leading practices in workforce planning. We also compared the information across agencies to determine the level of consistency. We supplemented the documentation provided by the agencies with interviews we conducted with agency officials in information security, training, and human resources.

To determine the status of governmentwide cybersecurity workforce initiatives, we first identified governmentwide initiatives based on interviews with subject matter experts at federal agencies and private organizations, and a review of publicly released information on the initiatives. For the initiatives identified, we reviewed plans, performance measures, and status reports. We also interviewed officials at agencies responsible for these initiatives, such as NIST, OPM, the National Science Foundation, and OMB. We assessed the status and plans of these efforts against our prior work on strategic planning, training and development, and efficient government operations.

As part of our presentation of governmentwide cybersecurity workforce initiatives, we presented the results of the IT Workforce Capability Assessment administered by the CIO Council. While we did not independently assess the quality of the survey and results, we examined the data to identify any obvious problems with reasonableness and accuracy, and discussed our presentation of the data with officials responsible for the survey results. We determined these data were sufficiently reliable for the purposes of this report.

We conducted this performance audit from December 2010 to November 2011 in accordance with generally accepted government auditing standards. Those standards require that we plan and perform the audit to obtain sufficient, appropriate evidence to provide a reasonable basis for our findings and conclusions based on our audit objectives. We believe that the evidence obtained provides a reasonable basis for our findings and conclusions based on our audit objectives.

End Notes

[1] President Barack Obama, "Cyberspace Policy Review: Assuring a Trusted and Resilient Information and Communications Infrastructure" (Washington, D.C.: May 29, 2009).
[2] See GAO, *High Risk Series: An Update*, GAO-1 1-278 (Washington, D.C.: February 2011).
[3] GAO-1 1-278.
[4] General Keith B. Alexander, in a statement before the House Committee on Armed Services, Subcommittee on Emerging Threats and Capabilities, Washington, D.C., March 16, 2011.

[5] Partnership for Public Service and Booz Allen Hamilton, *Cyber In-Security Strengthening the Federal Cybersecurity Workforce* (Washington, D.C.: July 22, 2009).

[6] Center for Strategic and International Studies, *A Human Capital Crisis in Cybersecurity—Technical Proficiency Matters* (Washington, D.C.: April 2010).

[7] Commerce Office of Inspector General, *Commerce Should Take Steps to Strengthen Its IT Security Workforce*, CAR-1 9569-1 (Washington D.C.: September 2009).

[8] DHS Office of Inspector General, *U.S. Computer Emergency Readiness Team Makes Progress in Securing Cyberspace, but Challenges Remain*, OIG-1 0-94 (Washington D.C.: June 7, 2010).

[9] Alexander statement.

[10] Justice Office of the Inspector General, *The Federal Bureau of Investigation's Ability to Address the National Security Cyber Intrusion Threat*, Audit Report 1 1-22 (Washington D.C.: April 2011).

[11] GAO, *Human Capital: Key Principles for Effective Strategic Workforce Planning*, GAO- 04-39 (Washington D.C.: Dec. 11, 2003); *A Model Of Strategic Human Capital Management*, GAO-02-373SP (Washington D.C.: Mar. 15, 2002); *Human Capital: A Self- Assessment Checklist for Agency Leaders*, GAO/OCG-00-14G (Washington D.C.: September 2000); OPM, *Human Capital Assessment and Accountability Framework— Systems, Standards, and Metrics* (http://www.opm .gov/hcaaf_resource_center/).

[12] 5 CFR § 250.203 (2011).

[13] GAO-04-39.

[14] A competency model identifies and describes a set of characteristics for a job description that are essential to effective performance of that position.

[15] OMB, *M-11-29: Chief Information Officer Authorities* (Washington, D.C.: Aug. 8, 2011).

[16] Title III of the E-Government Act of 2002, Pub. L. No. 107-347, Dec. 17, 2002; OMB, *Fiscal Year 2010 Report to Congress on the Implementation of the Federal Information Security Management Act of 2002* (Washington, D.C.: Mar. 1, 2011).

[17] An FTE is the number of total hours worked divided by the maximum number of compensable hours in a work year. For example, if the work year is defined as 2,080 hours, then one worker occupying a paid full time job all year would consume one FTE. Two persons working for 1,040 hours each would consume one FTE between the two of them.

[18] GAO, *Defense Department Cyber Efforts: DOD Faces Challenges in Its Cyber Activities*, GAO-1 1-75 (Washington D.C.: July 25, 2011).

[19] GAO-04-39 and GAO, *Comptroller's Forum, High Performing Organizations: Metrics, Means, and Mechanisms for Achieving High Performance in the 21st Century Public Management Environment*, GAO-04-343SP (Washington, D.C.: Feb. 13, 2004).

[20] The CIO Council is chaired by the Deputy Director for Management of OMB and has members from 28 federal agencies.

[21] Department of Commerce, National Institute of Standards and Technology, Special Publication 800-37 Revision 1, *Guide for Applying the Risk Management Framework to Federal Information Systems* (Gaithersburg, Md.: 2010).

[22] Department of Defense, DOD 8570.01-M, "Information Assurance Workforce Improvement Program" (Dec. 19, 2005).

[23] GAO, *Human Capital: Opportunities to Improve Executive Agencies' Hiring Processes*, GAO-03-450 (Washington, D.C.: May 30, 2003).

[24] GAO/OCG-00-1 4G.

[25] GAO-03-450.

[26] The White House, Office of the Press Secretary, "Presidential Memorandum–Improving the Federal Recruitment and Hiring Process," Washington, D.C., May 11, 2010.

[27] Federal employees can be hired under several different hiring authorities, including competitive service (the standard hiring authority), excepted service, and direct hire authority. Each authority has different rules and regulations governing the selection of

candidates, with the rules for excepted service and direct hire intended to make it easier or faster for agencies to hire personnel under certain circumstances.

[28] Presidential Memorandum–"Improving the Federal Recruitment and Hiring Process," May 11, 2010.

[29] Category rating allows hiring managers to select from among all candidates who are grouped in the highest-quality category for rating applications. The "rule of three," which was often used previously, limits hiring managers to selecting potential hires from only among the three highest-rated candidates.

[30] GAO, *High-Risk Series: An Update*, GAO-05-207 (Washington, D.C.: January 2005), and *DOD Personnel Clearances: Comprehensive Timeliness Reporting, Complete Clearance Documentation, and Quality Measures Are Needed to Further Improve the Clearance Process*, GAO-09-400 (Washington, D.C.: May 19, 2009).

[31] GAO, *Personnel Security Clearances: Progress Has Been Made to Improve Timeliness, but Continued Oversight Is Needed to Sustain Momentum*, GAO-1 1-65 (Washington, D.C.: Nov. 19. 2010), and GAO-11-278.

[32] According to OPM, an agency may also use additional incentives, such as special pay rates and recruitment, retention, and relocation incentives in excess of predefined limits by seeking approval from OPM.

[33] 5 CFR § 575.112, 5 CFR § 575.212, 5 CFR § 575.312.

[34] GAO, *Human Capital: Continued Opportunities Exist for FDA and OPM to Improve Oversight of Recruitment, Relocation, and Retention Incentives*, GAO-1 0-226 (Washington, D.C.: Jan. 22, 2010).

[35] OPM, *Recruitment, Relocation and Retention Incentives Calendar Year 2009 Report to the Congress* (Washington, D.C.: August 2011).

[36] GAO-10-226.

[37] OPM, *Plan to Improve the Administration and Oversight of Recruitment, Relocation and Retention Incentives* (Washington, D.C.: Feb. 3, 2010).

[38] In commenting on a draft of this report, OPM stated that when the regulations are finalized they are likely to contain criteria for these annual reviews similar to criteria in existing OPM regulations.

[39] GAO-03-450; National Commission on the Public Service, *Urgent Business for America— Revitalizing The Federal Government for The 21st Century*, (Washington, D.C.: Jan. 2003); and OPM, *A Fresh Start for Federal Pay: The Case for Modernization* (Washington, D.C.: April 2002). In addition, in commenting on a draft of this report, OPM stated that the Director of OPM has taken more recent steps toward improved performance management through participation in governmentwide working groups

[40] GAO, *Human Capital: A Guide for Assessing Strategic Training and Development Efforts in the Federal Government*, GAO-04-546G (Washington D.C.: March 2004), and OPM, *Human Resources Flexibiities and Authorities in the Federal Government* (Washington, D.C.: January 2008).

[41] In January 2008, President Bush issued National Security Presidential Directive 54/Homeland Security Presidential Directive 23, establishing the Comprehensive National Cybersecurity Initiative, a set of projects aimed at safeguarding executive branch information systems by reducing potential vulnerabilities, protecting against intrusion attempts, and anticipating future threats.

[42] The Federal Information Systems Security Educators' Association is an organization of federal information systems security professionals that provides a forum for the exchange of information on federal information systems security awareness, training, and education programs.

[43] NIST Special Publication 800-37 Revision 1; Special Publication 800-16 Revision 1, *Information Security Training Requirements: A Role-and Performance-Based Model* (draft) (Gaithersburg, Md.: 2009); Special Publication 800-50, *Building an Information Technology Security Awareness and Training Program* (Gaithersburg, Md.: 2003).

[44] The series were 2210, Information Technology Management; 0855, Electrical Engineering; 0854, Computer Engineering; and 0391, Telecommunications Engineering.

[45] GAO, *Opportunities to Reduce Potential Duplication in Government Programs, Save Tax Dollars, and Enhance Revenue*, GAO-1 1-31 8SP (Washington, D.C.: Mar. 1, 2011).

[46] GAO, *Human Capital: Selected Agencies' Experiences and Lessons Learned in Designing Training and Development Programs*, GAO-04-291 (Washington, D.C.: Jan. 30, 2004).

[47] GAO-11-318SP.

[48] 40 U.S.C. § 11315(c)(3).

[49] GAO-04-291.

In: Federal Cybersecurity Planning
Editors: K. C. Moore and M. D. Taylor

ISBN 978-1-61942-769-3
© 2012 Nova Science Publishers, Inc.

Chapter 2

CYBERSECURITY: KEY CHALLENGES NEED TO BE ADDRESSED TO IMPROVE RESEARCH AND DEVELOPMENT[*]

United States Government Accountability Office

WHY GAO DID THIS STUDY

Computer networks and infrastructures, on which the United States and much of the world rely to communicate and conduct business, contain vulnerabilities that can leave them susceptible to unauthorized access, disruption, or attack. Investing in research and development (R&D) is essential to protect critical systems and to enhance the cybersecurity of both the government and the private sector. Federal law has called for improvements in cybersecurity R&D, and, recently, President Obama has stated that advancing R&D is one of his administration's top priorities for improving cybersecurity.

GAO was asked to determine the key challenges in enhancing national-level cybersecurity R&D efforts among the federal government and private companies. To do this, GAO consulted with officials from relevant federal agencies and experts from private sector companies and academic institutions as well as analyzed key documents, such as agencies' research plans.

---

[*] This is an edited, reformatted and augmented version of a United States Government Accountability Office Report to Congressional Requesters, GAO-10-466 dated, June 2010.

WHAT GAO RECOMMENDS

GAO is recommending that the Director of OSTP direct NITRD to exercise its leadership responsibilities by taking several actions, including developing a national agenda, and establishing and utilizing a mechanism to keep track of federal cybersecurity R&D funding. OSTP agreed with GAO's recommendation and provided details on planned actions.

WHAT GAO FOUND

Several major challenges impede efforts to improve cybersecurity R&D. Among the most critical challenges are the following:

Establishing a prioritized national R&D agenda. While R&D that is in support of specific agencies' missions is important, it is also essential that national research efforts be strategically guided by an ordered set of national-level R&D goals. Additionally, it is critical that cyberspace security research efforts are prioritized across all sectors to ensure that national goals are addressed. Accordingly, the National Strategy to Secure Cyberspace recommended that the Office of Science and Technology Policy (OSTP) coordinate the development of an annual cybersecurity research agenda that includes near-term (1-3 years), mid-term (3-5 years), and long-term (5 years or longer) goals. Although OSTP has taken initial steps toward developing such an agenda, one does not currently exist. OSTP and Office of Management and Budget officials stated that they believe an agenda is contained in existing documents; however, these documents are either outdated or lack appropriate detail. Without a current national cybersecurity R&D agenda, the nation is at risk that agencies and private sector companies may focus on their individual priorities, which may not be the most important national research priorities.

Strengthening leadership. While officials within OSTP's Subcommittee on Networking and Information Technology Research and Development (NITRD)—a multiagency coordination body that is primarily responsible for providing leadership in coordinating cybersecurity R&D—have played a facilitator role in coordinating cybersecurity R&D efforts within the federal government, they have not led agencies in a strategic direction. NITRD's lack of leadership has been noted by many experts as well as by a presidential advisory committee that reported that federal cybersecurity R&D efforts should be focused, coordinated, and overseen by a central body. Until NITRD exercises its leadership responsibilities, federal agencies will lack overall direction for cybersecurity R&D.

Tracking R&D funding and establishing processes for the public and private sectors to share key R&D information. Despite a congressional mandate to develop a governmentwide repository that tracks federally funded R&D, including R&D related to cybersecurity, such a repository is not currently in place. Additionally, the government does not have a process to foster the kinds of relationships necessary for coordination between the public and private sectors. While NITRD hosted a major conference last year that brought together public, private, and academic experts, this was a one-time event, and, according to experts, next steps remain unclear. Without a mechanism to track all active and completed cybersecurity R&D initiatives, federal researchers and developers as well as private companies lack essential information about ongoing and completed R&D. Moreover, without a process for industry and government to share cybersecurity R&D information, the nation is at risk of having unforeseen gaps.

ABBREVIATIONS

CNCI	Comprehensive National Cybersecurity Initiative
CSIA IWG	Cyber Security and Information Assurance Interagency Working Group
CSIS	Center for Strategic and International Studies
DARPA	Defense Advanced Research Projects Agency
DHS	Department of Homeland Security
DOD	Department of Defense
DOE	Department of Energy
IT	information technology
IT-SCC	Information Technology Sector Coordinating Council
NIST	National Institute of Standards and Technology
NITRD	Subcommittee on Networking and Information Technology Research and Development
NSA	National Security Agency
NSF	National Science Foundation
NSTC	National Science and Technology Council

OMB	Office of Management and Budget
OSTP	Office of Science and Technology Policy
PCAST	President's Council of Advisors on Science and Technology
PITAC	President's Information Technology Advisory Committee
R&D	research and development
RaDiUS	Research and Development in the U.S. (database)
SCORE	Special Cyber Operations Research and Engineering

June 3, 2010

The Honorable Bennie G. Thompson
Chairman
Committee on Homeland Security
House of Representatives

The Honorable Yvette D. Clarke
Chairwoman
Subcommittee on Emerging Threats, Cybersecurity, and Science and Technology
Committee on Homeland Security
House of Representatives

Dramatic increases in computer interconnectivity, especially in the use of the Internet, continue to revolutionize the way that our government, our nation, and much of the world communicate and conduct business. However, computers, networks, and their infrastructures are not always designed with security in mind. As a result, public and private systems that support critical operations and infrastructures of the federal government can have significant vulnerabilities[1] that can be exploited by malicious users to gain unauthorized access to systems and obtain sensitive information, commit fraud, disrupt operations, or launch attacks against Web sites.

Because of concerns about these malicious attacks from individuals and groups, it is essential that the United States protect its existing critical systems and at the same time work to get ahead of its adversaries by ensuring that future generations of technology will position the United States to better protect its critical systems from attack. As such, we have designated protecting the federal government's information systems as a high-risk area.[2] Research in cybersecurity[3] technology is essential to creating a broader range of choices and more robust tools for building secure, networked computer systems in the federal government and in the private sector. Furthermore, over the past two decades, federal law and policy have called for improvements in the research and development (R&D) of cybersecurity tools and techniques. In May 2009, President Obama announced that advancing R&D is one of his administration's top five priorities for improving cybersecurity.

This report responds to your request that we conduct a review of the nation's current cybersecurity-related R&D efforts. Specifically, our objective was to determine the key challenges to enhancing national-level cybersecurity R&D efforts among the federal government and private companies.

To address this objective, we identified experts from the public and private sectors that conduct or coordinate cybersecurity R&D, including 7 government agencies/entities—the Departments of Defense (DOD), Homeland Security (DHS), and Energy (DOE) and the National Science Foundation (NSF), the National Institute of Standards and Technology (NIST), the Office of Management and Budget (OMB), and the Office of Science and Technology Policy (OSTP); 24 private sector entities; and 3 academic institutions (see app. I for the complete list). To obtain information on the key R&D challenges that these entities face, we analyzed documentation, such as agencies' research plans and cybersecurity reports, and interviewed federal and industry experts. We then aggregated the identified challenges and validated the top challenges by asking the experts to rank the challenges in order of importance. Appendix I contains further details of our objective, scope, and methodology.

We conducted this performance audit from June 2009 to June 2010, in accordance with generally accepted government auditing standards. Those standards require that we plan and perform the audit to obtain sufficient, appropriate evidence to provide a reasonable basis for our findings and conclusions based on our audit objective. We believe that the evidence obtained provides a reasonable basis for our findings and conclusions based on our audit objective.

BACKGROUND

The speed, functionality, and accessibility that create the enormous benefits of the computer age can, if not properly controlled, allow individuals and organizations to easily eavesdrop on or interfere with computer operations from remote locations for mischievous or malicious purposes, including fraud or sabotage. As public and private organizations use computer systems to transfer more and greater amounts of money, sensitive economic and commercial information, and critical defense and intelligence information, the likelihood increases that malicious individuals will attempt to penetrate current security technologies, disrupt or disable our nation's critical infrastructures, and use sensitive and critical information for malicious purposes.

Because the threats have persisted and grown, in January 2008, the President began implementing a series of initiatives—commonly referred to as the Comprehensive National Cybersecurity Initiative (CNCI)—aimed primarily at improving DHS and other federal agencies' efforts to protect against intrusion attempts and anticipate future threats.[4] Two of these initiatives are related to improving cybersecurity R&D—one is aimed at improving the coordination of federal cybersecurity R&D, and the other is aimed at developing a plan for advancing the United States' R&D in high-risk, high-return areas. We recently reported that CNCI faces significant challenges, including defining roles and responsibilities and coordinating efforts.[5]

Numerous Entities Are Involved in the Cybersecurity Research and Development Arena

Several federal entities oversee and aim to coordinate federal cybersecurity research; private entities have structures in place aimed at coordinating research; and numerous federal agencies and private companies fund or conduct this research.

Federal Oversight and Coordination of Cybersecurity R&D

OSTP and OMB, both in the Executive Office of the President, are responsible for providing high-level oversight of federal R&D, including cybersecurity. OSTP promotes the work of the National Science and Technology Council, which prepares R&D strategies that are intended to be coordinated across federal agencies. The council operates through its committees, subcommittees, and interagency working groups, which coordinate activities related to specific science and technology disciplines.

Table 1 contains a brief description of the roles and responsibilities of the federal organizations and groups involved in the oversight and coordination of cybersecurity research.

Table 1. Federal Organizations Involved in the Oversight and Coordination of Cybersecurity Research

Organization	Description
President's Council of Advisors on Science and Technology (PCAST)	Executive Order 13226 established PCAST in September 2001. Under this order, PCAST was established to advise the President on matters involving science and technology policy and assist the National Science and Technology Council in securing private sector involvement in its activities. The council's members are appointed by the President and originate from industry, education, and research institutions and other nongovernmental organizations. The Director of OSTP serves as a co-chair for the council.
President's Information Technology Advisory Committee (PITAC)	PITAC is made up of industry and academic experts appointed by the President to provide independent expert advice to the President, Congress, and federal agencies on networking and information technology R&D. In September 2005, Executive Order 13385 reassigned the roles and responsibilities of PITAC to PCAST.
National Security Council	The council is the President's principal forum for considering national security and foreign policy matters with his senior national security advisors and cabinet officials. The council is chaired by the President. The Cybersecurity Coordinator and Director of National Intelligence both work with the council.
Cybersecurity Office/U.S. Cybersecurity Coordinator	In December 2009, the President created the Cybersecurity Office within the National Security Council and appointed a U.S. Cybersecurity Coordinator. The coordinator is intended to work closely with the federal Chief Information Officer, the federal Chief Technology Officer, and the National Economic Council.
Office of the Director of National Intelligence	The Office of the Director of National Intelligence was established in April 2005. The head of this office serves as the President's principal intelligence advisor and is intended to establish the intelligence community's priorities with clear and measurable goals and objectives as well as provide leadership on cross-cutting intelligence community issues. According to OSTP officials, this office provides technical and administrative support to the Special Cyber Operations Research and Engineering Interagency Working Group.

Table 1. (Continued)

Organization	Description
Office of Management and Budget (OMB)	The E-Government Act of 2002 mandated that OMB ensure the development and maintenance of a governmentwide repository and Web site that integrates information about federally funded R&D, including R&D related to cybersecurity. Furthermore, the Director of OMB and the Director of OSTP jointly release an annual memorandum to the heads of executive departments and agencies that specifies high-level R&D budget priorities, one of which is to protect the nation's information infrastructure.
Office of Science and Technology Policy (OSTP)	OSTP serves as a primary advisor to the President for policy formation and budget development on all questions in which science and technology are important elements. The office also leads an interagency effort to develop and implement science and technology policies and budgets that are coordinated across federal agencies.
OSTP's National Science and Technology Council (NSTC)	NSTC, established in 1993, is the principal means for the administration to coordinate science and technology policy among the diverse entities that make up the federal R&D enterprise. OSTP works through NSTC to develop strategies that are coordinated across federal agencies. The council operates through its committees, which include the Committee on Homeland and National Security and the Committee on Technology, among others. Each committee oversees a number of subcommittees and interagency working groups focused on science and technology.
NSTC's Committee on Technology	The Committee on Technology addresses policy matters that cut across agency boundaries and provides a formal mechanism for interagency policy coordination and balanced and comprehensive technology R&D programs. Senior-level representatives from federal departments and agencies comprise the committee. The committee is currently co-chaired by the U.S. Chief Information Officer in OMB and the Chief Technology Officer in OSTP. Several other agencies or components are members of the committee, including the Departments of Homeland Security (DHS), Defense (DOD), Justice, Transportation, and the Treasury; the Central Intelligence Agency; the National Security Agency (NSA); and the Office of the Cyber Security Officer from the National Security Council.

Organization	Description
The Committee on Technology's Subcommittee on Networking and Information Technology Research and Development (NITRD)	NITRD is a multiagency coordination program that seeks to ensure continued U.S. technological leadership and accelerate deployment of advanced and experimental information technologies. Subcommittee members include representatives from 15 federal agencies or components, including the National Science Foundation (NSF), DOD, NSA, and National Institute of Standards and Technology (NIST). NITRD is responsible for coordinating the planning, budgeting, and assessment of activities of a multiagency federal NITRD program. This program was chartered under the High-Performance Computing Act of 1991, as amended by the Next Generation Internet Research Act of 1998 and the America COMPETES Act of 2007, to help sustain U.S. leadership in cutting-edge science, engineering, and technology through investments from federal agencies involved in information technology R&D.[a]
National Coordination Office (NCO) for NITRD	NCO is responsible for providing technical and administrative support for the Subcommittee on Networking and Information Technology Research and Development and interagency activities of the NITRD program. This includes helping identify research needs by coordinating interagency meetings as well as conferences and workshops with academia and industry. This office is to aid information dissemination by publishing reports, including reports produced by the PITAC, and the annual supplements to the President's budget.
Senior Steering Group for Cyber Security	In Spring 2008, a senior steering group was created and added to NITRD, which is intended to provide overall leadership and cybersecurity R&D coordination(CNCI Coordination Plan. The steering group's membership includes the co-chair for NITRD; the director of NCO; and senior representatives of agencies, such as DOD, DHS, National Security Agency, NIST, OSTP, and OMB. Additionally, the group is intended to facilitate closer interaction between classified and unclassified R&D. Accordingly, this group's membership also overlaps with the Special Cyber Operations Research and Engineering Interagency Working Group.
Cyber Security and Information	CSIA IWG was chartered in August 2005 to facilitate greater coordination of federal cybersecurity R&D.

Table 1. (Continued)

Organization	Description
Assurance Interagency Working Group (CSIA IWG)	The working group reports to NITRD and is responsible for facilitating interagency program planning, developing and periodically updating an interagency roadmap, developing recommendations for establishing federal policies and priorities, summarizing annual activities for the NITRD program's supplement to the President's budget, and identifying potential opportunities for collaboration and coordination. Members include NSF, DOD's research organizations, NSA, the Defense Advanced Research Projects Agency, and NIST. Other participants include the Central Intelligence Agency; the Environmental Protection Agency; the National Aeronautics and Space Administration; the National Institutes of Health; and the Departments of Homeland Security, Energy, Justice, State, Transportation, and the Treasury.
Special Cyber Operations Research and Engineering (SCORE) Interagency Working Group	SCORE was created in Spring 2008 and is intended to work in parallel to the CSIA IWG to coordinate classified cybersecurity R&D. It is operated under OSTP and the Director for National Intelligence. Representatives from the SCORE and CSIA IWG participate together in the Senior Steering Group for Cyber Security.

Source: GAO analysis of Executive Office of the President information.
[a] The High-Performance Computing Act of 1991, Pub. L. No. 102-194, 105 Stat. 1595 (Dec. 9, 1991), was amended by the Next Generation Internet Research Act of 1998, Pub. L. No. 105-305, 112 Stat. 2919 (Oct. 28, 1998), and the America COMPETES Act, Pub. L. No. 110-69, 121 Stat. 572 (Aug. 9, 2007).

Private Sector Cybersecurity R&D Coordination

The private sector also has cybersecurity R&D working groups aimed at better coordinating R&D. Under an existing information-sharing framework within a plan referred to as the *National Infrastructure Protection Plan*,[6] two Sector Coordinating Councils, Financial Services and Information Technology have R&D working groups. These groups are composed of representatives from companies, associations, and other key sector participants to coordinate strategic activities and communicate broad sector member views associated with cybersecurity R&D throughout their sectors. Specifically, these working groups are charged with conducting annual reviews of R&D initiatives in their sectors and recommending updates to those priorities based on changes in technology, threats, vulnerabilities, and risk.

Federal Agencies and Private Companies Fund or Conduct Cybersecurity R&D

Five agencies—NSF, DHS, DOD, DOE, and NIST—fund and conduct much of the government's cybersecurity R&D.

According to agency officials, NSF's main cybersecurity R&D program is the Trustworthy Computing Program. This program is to support research and education activities that explore novel frameworks, theories, and approaches toward secure and privacy-preserving systems. According to the Subcommittee on Networking and Information Technology Research and Development's (NITRD) supplement to the 2011 budget, NSF's budget was approximately $71.4 million for cybersecurity R&D.

DHS's R&D efforts are aimed at countering threats to the homeland by making evolutionary improvements to current capabilities and developing revolutionary new capabilities. DHS's cybersecurity R&D program resides in the agency's Science and Technology Directorate. DHS has created R&D tools and made them accessible to the broader research community, such as an experimental research testing environment and a research data repository. In November 2009, DHS issued *A Roadmap for Cybersecurity Research*, which was an attempt to establish a foundation on which a national R&D agenda could be built. Furthermore, it was intended to provide detailed R&D agendas related to specific cybersecurity problems.[7]

Several agencies within DOD have cybersecurity R&D programs. The department's Defense Research and Engineering organization within the Office of the Director provides coordination and oversight and supports certain cybersecurity research activities directly. The office is responsible for DOD's science and technology activities as well as for oversight of research and engineering. Although the department's research organizations (e.g., the Office of Naval Research, the Army Research Laboratory, and the Air Force Research Laboratory) have cybersecurity programs, the largest investments within its cybersecurity R&D are with the Defense Advanced Research Projects Agency (DARPA) and the National Security Agency (NSA). DARPA is the central R&D organization for the department, and its cybersecurity R&D budget for fiscal year 2010 is approximately $144 million.[8] Its mission is to identify revolutionary, high-risk, high-payoff technologies of interest to the military, then to support the development of these technologies through transition. NSA also performs extensive cybersecurity research. Its research programs focus on high-speed encryption and certain defense capabilities, among other things. For fiscal year 2010, the agency's budget was approximately $29 million for cybersecurity R&D. The research is conducted and supported by its National Information Assurance Research Group. In addition to DARPA and NSA, approximately $70 million was budgeted for fiscal year 2010 to the Office of the Secretary of Defense and other research organizations within DOD for additional cybersecurity R&D.

DOE also conducts and funds cybersecurity R&D. Nearly all of DOE's cybersecurity R&D investments are directed toward short-term applications. This work is conducted principally at the national laboratories. DOE reported to NITRD that it had spent $3.5 million on cybersecurity R&D for fiscal year 2010, and requested the same amount for fiscal year 2011. Additionally, DOE conducts cybersecurity R&D for other departments, such as DOD.

NIST's cybersecurity research program is multidisciplinary and focuses on a range of long-term and applied R&D. NIST also conducts security research in support of future standards and guidelines. NIST's fiscal year 2010 budget for cybersecurity was about $29 million. The agency also receives funding from other agencies, such as DHS, the Department of Transportation and the General Services Administration—to work on projects that are consistent with its cybersecurity mission.

In addition, many private sector companies pursue government grants or contracts to conduct cybersecurity R&D on behalf of the government, or they independently self-fund cybersecurity research. The private sector generally conducts cybersecurity R&D in areas with commercial viability, which are focused on developing products to help their customers better secure their systems and networks. For example, representatives from one private sector company stated that they have set up unused computers that attempt to attract hackers for the purpose of analyzing the attacker. Another company is conducting R&D related to the Internet's architecture. According to private sector officials, cybersecurity R&D does not necessarily have to be conducted by large companies; some small companies have made large contributions.

Various Entities Have Issued Guidance on Federal Cybersecurity R&D

Various public and private sector entities have issued reports that provide guidance and make recommendations for improvements in the nation's activities related to specific aspects of cybersecurity, including R&D. The following key reports offer guidance and direction related to cybersecurity R&D:

- In February 2003, the White House's *The National Strategy to Secure Cyberspace* identified five national priorities, one of which includes reducing cyberspace threats and vulnerabilities.[9] As part of this priority, the strategy tasked the Director of OSTP with coordinating the development of a federal government R&D agenda for cybersecurity and updating it on an annual basis.
- In February 2005, the President's Information Technology Advisory Committee (PITAC) recommended several changes in the federal government's cybersecurity R&D portfolio.[10] One of the report's recommendations was to strengthen coordination and oversight of federal cybersecurity efforts.
- The President's Council of Advisors on Science and Technology (PCAST) found in its 2007 report, entitled *Leadership Under Challenge: Information Technology R&D in a Competitive World*, that the existing federal networking and information technology R&D portfolio was unbalanced in favor of low-risk, small-scale, and short-term efforts.[11] The council recommended that federal agencies increase support for larger- scale, longer-term R&D.
- In December 2008, the Center for Strategic and International Studies (CSIS) Commission on Cybersecurity for the 44th Presidency issued a series of recommendations for a comprehensive national approach to securing cyberspace.[12] As part of the review, CSIS recommended the creation of a new National Office of Cyberspace, which would work with OSTP to provide overall coordination of cybersecurity R&D.
- The Institute for Information Infrastructure Protection's report, entitled *National Cyber Security: Research and Development Challenges Related to Economics, Physical Infrastructure, and Human Behavior*, stated that a national cybersecurity research agenda was urgently needed that prioritizes problems; encourages and tracks

innovative approaches; and provides a pipeline of short-, medium-, and long-term projects.[13]

- The National Security and Homeland Security Councils' report, entitled *Cyberspace Policy Review: Assuring a Trusted and Resilient Information and Communications Infrastructure*, recommended that a framework for R&D be developed.[14] The report also recommended that the administration appoint a cybersecurity policy official to coordinate the nation's cybersecurity policies and activities. Accordingly, as we have previously mentioned, in December 2009, President Obama appointed a national Cybersecurity Coordinator. Among many things, this official is tasked with updating the national cybersecurity strategy. We have a review under way that is assessing the implementation status of the recommendations that were made in the *Cyberspace Policy Review*.
- In November 2009, DHS issued a report entitled *A Roadmap for Cybersecurity Research*, which identifies critical needs and gaps in 11 cybersecurity research areas.

GAO Has Made Recommendations to Improve Cybersecurity R&D

In addition to the recent cybersecurity reports, we have reported on the importance of furthering cybersecurity R&D. Specifically, in September 2006, we reported on actions taken by federal entities to improve the oversight and coordination of federal cybersecurity R&D activities.[15] We found that federal entities had taken several important steps to improve the oversight and coordination of federal cybersecurity R&D; however, a federal cybersecurity research agenda had not yet been developed. Furthermore, the federal government's R&D repositories did not contain information about all of the federally funded cybersecurity research projects. As a result, we recommended, among other things, that the Director of OSTP establish firm timelines for the completion of the federal cybersecurity R&D agenda, which includes near-term, mid-term, and long-term research. We also recommended that the Director of OMB issue guidance to agencies on reporting information about federally funded cybersecurity R&D projects to the governmentwide repositories. Although OMB and OSTP have taken initial steps, the agencies have not fully implemented these recommendations.

Additionally, in March 2009, we testified on key improvements needed to strengthen the national cybersecurity strategy. Based on input we received from expert panels, we identified 12 key improvements that are essential to enhancing the strategy and our national cybersecurity posture.[16] One of these improvements was placing greater emphasis on cybersecurity R&D, including consideration of how to better coordinate government and private sector efforts.

KEY CHALLENGES TO IMPROVING NATIONAL CYBERSECURITY R&D EFFORTS

While efforts are under way by OSTP, NITRD, and individual agencies to improve cybersecurity R&D, significant challenges remain. We identified, through input from experts from relevant federal, private, and academic organizations, six major challenges that are impeding efforts to improve cybersecurity R&D.

Lack of a Prioritized National Cybersecurity R&D Agenda

According to key expert bodies, a national cybersecurity R&D agenda should embody several characteristics. Specifically, according to the *National Strategy to Secure Cyberspace*, a national R&D agenda should include near-term (1 to 3 years), mid-term (3 to 5 years), and long-term (5 years and longer) goals. Additionally, an agenda should include national- level R&D priorities that go beyond goals specific to agencies' and companies' missions. It is also essential that cyberspace security research efforts are ranked across all sectors and funding sources to ensure that national goals are addressed. Additionally, according to the Institute for Information Infrastructure Protection, it is important that an agenda include perspectives from both the public and private sectors. An agenda should also specify timelines and milestones for conducting cybersecurity R&D activities. Moreover, in 2006, we recommended that OSTP develop a federal cybersecurity R&D agenda that includes near-term, mid-term, and long-term research.[17] Additionally, pursuant to the High-Performance Computing Act of 1991, as amended by the Next Generation Internet Research Act of 1998 and the America COMPETES Act of 2007, NITRD is responsible for setting goals and priorities for cybersecurity R&D.

However, despite its legal responsibility and our past recommendations, NITRD has not created a prioritized national or federal R&D agenda. Officials from DOD, DOE, and DHS indicated that there is a lack of a prioritized cybersecurity R&D agenda. Furthermore, the aggregated ranked responses from 24 cybersecurity R&D private and academic experts we contacted indicated that the lack of a prioritized national R&D agenda is the top challenge that they believe should be addressed.[18]

While officials from NITRD and OMB stated that they consider the following key documents to comprise a national R&D agenda, these documents do not constitute, whether taken collectively or separately, a prioritized national agenda:

- NITRD's 2006 Cyber Security and Information Assurance Working Group's *Federal Plan for Cyber Security and Information Assurance R&D*: As we have previously reported, this plan was intended to be the first step toward developing a federal agenda for cybersecurity research, which provides baseline information about ongoing federal R&D activities; however, mid-term and long-term cybersecurity research goals were not defined. Furthermore, the plan does not specify timelines and milestones for conducting R&D activities, nor does it assign responsibility for implementation. Additionally, this plan was published in 2006, and many experts indicated that it is outdated. For example, NSF officials, who were co-developers of the plan, stated that the document does not take into account new types of threats that have appeared in the past 4 years, and some of the issues identified in the 2006 report are less critical today. According to NITRD officials, this plan is intended to be a 5-year plan, and they do not plan to update it until 2012.
- The National Security and Homeland Security Councils' 2009 *Cyberspace Policy Review: Assuring a Trusted and Resilient Information and Communications Infrastructure*: This report presents relevant high-level challenges and recommendations for improvements that cover the spectrum of cybersecurity issues. However, according to NSF officials, the report does not contain sufficient detail related to R&D to be a research agenda. Furthermore, DHS officials stated that the *Cyberspace Policy Review* does not attempt to articulate a national-level R&D agenda.

- August 2009 OMB and OSTP memorandum, "Science and Technology Priorities for the FY 2011 Budget (M-09-27)": This memorandum also does not provide guidance on cybersecurity R&D priorities. As pointed out by DHS officials, this memorandum provides high-level points for consideration but does not provide a clear national cybersecurity R&D agenda. Moreover, DOD stated that the memorandum only provides general guidance for departments and agencies as they develop their overall science and technology programs.
- National Science and Technology Council's 2008 *Federal Plan for Advanced Networking and Research and Development*: This plan specifically focuses on establishing goals and time frames for enhancing networking capabilities, which includes enhancing networking security and reliability. However, networking is just one of several areas that need to be addressed in the cybersecurity R&D arena.

The private sector organizations and cybersecurity R&D experts that we contacted also did not consider the documents to constitute a national R&D agenda. Several private sector representatives stated that they exclusively use their own strategies to determine their cybersecurity R&D priorities.

According to NITRD's Cyber Security and Information Assurance Interagency Working Group (CSIA IWG) members, they have recently begun working on developing a framework that focuses on three main cybersecurity R&D themes. The DOD co-chair of CSIA IWG stated that he believes the framework will constitute a national cybersecurity R&D agenda. The three themes that comprise the framework are (1) supporting security policies and security services for different types of cyber space interactions; (2) deploying systems that are both diverse and changing, to increase complexity and costs for attackers and system resiliency; and (3) developing cybersecurity incentives to create foundations for cybersecurity markets, establish meaningful metrics, and promote economically sound and secure practices. NITRD officials stated that they expect the framework to be finalized in time for the 2012 budget submission. However, these three themes do not cover all of the priorities that should be included in a national cybersecurity R&D agenda. For example, among other things, issues such as global-scale identity management, which was identified by DHS as a top problem that needs to be addressed, and computer forensics, which was identified by the private sector and several key government reports as a major area needing government focus, are not included in this framework.

Beyond developing a federal plan as we have previously recommended, there is a need for a broader national cybersecurity R&D agenda. Until such an agenda is developed that (1) contains short-term, mid-term, and long-term priorities, (2) includes input from both public and private sectors, and (3) is consistent with the updated national cybersecurity strategy (when it is available), increased risk exists that agencies and private sector organizations will focus on their individual priorities for cybersecurity R&D, which may not be the most important national research priorities.

Lack of Leadership for Improving Federal Cybersecurity R&D Efforts

According to key expert bodies, leadership for improving cybersecurity in R&D is composed of several attributes. Specifically, PITAC indicated that federal cybersecurity R&D efforts should be focused, coordinated, and overseen by a central body. More specifically, the committee recommended that NITRD become the focal point for coordinating federal cybersecurity R&D efforts. Furthermore, according to CSIS, NITRD should lead the nation toward an aggressive research agenda. Additionally, our previous work has highlighted the need to define and agree on roles and responsibilities, including how an effort will be led. In doing so, the entities can clarify who will do what, organize their joint and individual efforts, and facilitate decision making.[19]

Although NITRD is primarily responsible for providing leadership in coordinating cybersecurity R&D, it has played a facilitator role, rather than leading agencies in a strategic direction toward a cybersecurity R&D agenda. Experts from 24 private sector and academic R&D entities ranked this challenge as the second most important cybersecurity R&D challenge, and officials from 2 federal agencies indicated that they agreed that there is a lack of government leadership. For example, 2 private sector experts stated that there is confusion about who in the government is leading the cybersecurity R&D area. Another private sector expert stated that while NITRD is playing a facilitator role, there is no central entity that is strategically leading cyber-security R&D in the federal government.

NITRD has intentionally decided to play a facilitator role. Specifically, NITRD carries out several activities, such as hosting monthly meetings in which agencies discuss their initiatives and compiling all of its participating agencies' cybersecurity R&D efforts and budgets; however, it generally does not make any specific decisions about how these efforts could be better coordinated. Recently, NITRD pointed to the National Cyber Leap Year initiative and the output from that initiative—CSIA IWG's cybersecurity R&D framework that is under development—as evidence of NITRD's leadership approach; however, this framework has not been completed.

Until NITRD exercises its leadership responsibilities, federal agencies will likely lack overall direction for cybersecurity R&D.

Lack of a Process for Sharing Key Information on R&D Initiatives between Federal Agencies and the Private Sector

We have previously emphasized the importance of establishing a process to ensure widespread and ongoing sharing of key cybersecurity-related information between federal agencies and private sector entities.[20] Additionally, according to the 2009 *Cyberspace Policy Review*, it is important that the federal government share cybersecurity R&D information with the private sector.

To improve R&D-related information sharing, in 2008 the Information Technology Sector Coordinating Council (IT-SCC) R&D working group proposed a framework to the Information Technology Government Coordinating Council and NITRD to establish a process for federal agencies and the private sector to share key information on R&D initiatives.[21] Approximately 2 years have passed since the IT-SCC made its proposal, and still no decision has been made on whether the government will pursue the working group's proposal, nor has the government developed an alternative approach to sharing key R&D information.

According to federal and private experts, key factors exist that reduce the private sector's and government's willingness to share information and trust each other with regard to researching and developing new cybersecurity technologies. Specifically, private sector officials stated that they are often unwilling to share details of their R&D with the government because they want to protect their intellectual property. On the government side, officials are concerned that the private sector is too focused on making a profit and may not necessarily conduct R&D in areas that require the most attention. Additionally, government and private sector officials indicated that the government does not have a process in place to communicate the results on completed federal R&D.

The private and public sectors share some cybersecurity R&D information, but such information-sharing generally occurs only on a project-by-project basis. For example, NSF's Industry University Cooperative Research Center initiative establishes centers to conduct research that is of interest to both industry and academia, and DOD's Small Business Innovation Research program funds R&D at small technology companies. However, according to federal and private sector experts, widespread and ongoing information-sharing generally does not occur. Without sharing such information, gaps in research among public and private sectors R&D is difficult to identify.

More recently, NITRD has taken steps to work more formally with the private sector and academia, such as hosting the National Cyber Leap Year Summit in August 2009, which aimed to bring together researchers and developers from the private and public sectors.

Nevertheless, without an ongoing process for industry and government to share cybersecurity R&D information, the nation could be at great risk of funding duplicative efforts or having gaps in needed R&D.

Limited Focus on Long-term, Complex Cybersecurity Research Projects

Several entities have emphasized that cybersecurity R&D should include long-term, complex projects. Specifically, the President's 2003 National Strategy to Secure Cyberspace indicated that it is important that the Director of OSTP develop a cybersecurity research agenda that includes long-term (5 years and longer) research. In 2006, we reported that researchers had indicated the need for long-term efforts, such as researching cybersecurity vulnerabilities, developing technological solutions, and transitioning research results into commercially available products.[22] Furthermore, in August 2007, PCAST recommended that federal agencies increase support for larger-scale, longer-term R&D.

While federal officials point to specific long-term cybersecurity R&D investments, such as DOD's development of a National Cyber Range[23] and NSF's Trustworthy Computing Program, OSTP has not established long-term research goals in a national agenda, the absence of which continues to plague the advancement of cybersecurity R&D. According to experts, one of the contributing factors to the limited focus on long-term R&D is that industry is focused on short-term, profit-generating R&D. Furthermore, experts stated that unless there is commercial viability, industry generally does not invest time or money. Another major contributing factor is that the federal government has been focused on obtaining and implementing new solutions immediately. For example, federal cybersecurity grants generally require grantees to deliver their research within a 3 year period, and, according to a cybersecurity expert at Purdue University, in many cases grantees are required to show the progress of their research within 6 months.

Although highly beneficial, short-term R&D, by definition, has limited focus and is not intended to independently tackle the more complex and fundamental problems related to cybersecurity, such as security problems related to the Internet's infrastructure. If the focus on cybersecurity R&D continues to be short-term and confined to our current technological environment, it may result in stunted research and growth, short-term fixes for systems, and networks that may not necessarily be developed with the most appropriate security.

Lack of a Sufficient Information Technology Human Capital Skill Base

Legislation and several key reports have stressed the importance of having sufficient cybersecurity education programs and an ample supply of qualified cybersecurity professionals. Specifically, the Cyber Security Research and Development Act stated that the United States needs to expand and improve the pool of information security professionals, including researchers, in the workforce.[24] In addition, the INFOSEC Research Council[25] reported that it is important that the United States enhance cybersecurity academic education and training.[26] In December 2008, the Center for Strategic and International Studies Commission on Cybersecurity for the 44th Presidency reported that the federal government needs to increase the supply of skilled workers and to create a career path (including training and advancement) for cyberspace specialists in the federal government.[27] Furthermore, one of the national Cybersecurity Coordinator's responsibilities is updating the national cybersecurity strategy, which addresses the cybersecurity human capital needs, among other things.

While several federal programs intended to promote cybersecurity-related professions exist today—such as NSF's Pathways to Revitalize Undergraduate Computing Education program and DOD's Science, Mathematics and

Research for Transformation Scholarship for Service program, which seek to develop a U.S. workforce with computing competencies—government officials and private sector experts agree that more can be done. For example, DHS officials indicated there is a shortage of cybersecurity R&D management officials. DOD officials indicated that more can be done to encourage personnel to pursue security degrees, and officials from DOE stated that it is very difficult to find highly qualified researchers with the requisite experience. Private sector experts voiced similar concerns, such as the need to cultivate talented people and the need for employees with more cybersecurity R&D experience.

Government officials and cybersecurity experts suggested that several factors have contributed to the lack of human capital expertise in the area of cybersecurity R&D. For example, federal officials and cybersecurity experts suggested that unclear career paths in cybersecurity have contributed to the lack of a sufficient skill base. Another expert stated that colleges or universities do not have the appropriate tools and products to adequately teach cybersecurity to students. While it has been 7 years since *The National Strategy to Secure Cyberspace* articulated plans for improving training and creating certifications, human capital weaknesses still exist.

Without obtaining information on the shortages in researchers in the cybersecurity field, it will be difficult for the national Cybersecurity Coordinator to update the national cybersecurity strategy with the appropriate cybersecurity human capital plans for addressing such weaknesses.

No Mechanism in Place That Identifies All Cybersecurity R&D Initiatives and Funding

Congress has recognized the importance of making available information on federal R&D funding for coordinating federal research activities and improving collaboration among those conducting federal R&D. To improve the methods by which government information is organized, preserved, and made accessible to the public, the E-Government Act of 2002 mandated that OMB ensure the development and maintenance of a governmentwide repository and Web site that integrates information about federally funded R&D, including R&D related to cybersecurity.[28] The Director of OMB delegated this responsibility to NSF.

As we have previously reported, NSF maintained a repository for federally funded R&D, known as the Research and Development in the U.S.

(RaDiUS) database; however, the database was incomplete and not fully populated.[29] Therefore, in 2006, we recommended that OMB issue guidance to agencies on reporting information about federally funded cybersecurity R&D projects to RaDiUS. OMB did not implement our recommendation. In 2008, the database was decommissioned because, according to a senior official at NSF, the data were incomplete, users had difficulty using it, and the database was built with antiquated technology. In March 2010, OMB officials stated that they are currently evaluating several repositories to replace RaDiUS as a centralized database to house all government-funded R&D programs, including cybersecurity R&D. While officials stated that they anticipate making a decision on a database by the end of fiscal year 2010, officials were unable to specify when a database would be in place that tracks all cybersecurity R&D information. Additionally, it is not clear how this fits into the overall coordination efforts for which NITRD is responsible.

Tracking funding that is allocated to classified R&D adds to the complexity of this challenge. For example, according to a DOD official, the majority of DOD's cybersecurity R&D is composed of either classified R&D or unclassified components of a program mixed with classified components, thereby rendering the entire program as classified. As such, it is difficult to identify the exact funding that is allocated to classified versus unclassified R&D.

There is currently no mechanism in place that identifies all cybersecurity R&D initiatives governmentwide and associated funding. DHS officials stated that it would be helpful to have a clearinghouse that they could use to view what activities are already being conducted by the government. In addition, a private sector expert stated that having a centralized database in place would improve coordination between the public and private sectors. However, challenges to maintaining such a mechanism exist. For example, an OSTP official indicated that it is difficult to develop and enforce policies for identifying specific funding as R&D. Additionally, the level of detail to be disclosed is also a factor because national security must also be protected.

However, without a mechanism to track all active and completed cybersecurity R&D initiatives, federal researchers and developers as well as private companies lack essential information about ongoing and completed R&D, thus increasing the likelihood of duplicative efforts, inefficient use of government funding, and lost collaboration opportunities. Additionally, with-out a complete understanding of how much each federal agency is spending on cybersecurity R&D, it may be difficult to make the appropriate resource allocation decisions.

CONCLUSION

OSTP and NITRD have recently taken steps to try to improve the coordination and oversight of cybersecurity R&D. However, key challenges still exist, and, until these challenges are addressed, the United States may continue to struggle in protecting and securing its critical systems and networks. Specifically, the absence of a national cybersecurity R&D agenda and leadership increases the risk that efforts will not reflect national priorities, key decisions will be postponed, and federal agencies will lack overall direction for their efforts. Furthermore, without sufficient attention to complex, long-term research projects and input on the current weaknesses and shortages in researchers in cybersecurity, the nation risks falling behind in cybersecurity and not being able to adequately protect its digital infrastructure. Finally, the lack of a mechanism to track all active and completed cybersecurity R&D initiatives and the lack of a process for sharing information among the public and private sectors may result in duplicative efforts or gaps in needed R&D.

RECOMMENDATION FOR EXECUTIVE ACTION

To help address the key cybersecurity R&D challenges, we are recommending that the Director of the Office of Science and Technology Policy, in conjunction with the national Cybersecurity Coordinator, direct the Subcommittee on Networking and Information Technology Research and Development to exercise its leadership responsibilities and take the following four actions:

- Establish a comprehensive national R&D agenda by expanding on the CSIA IWG framework and ensure that it
    - contains priorities for short-term, mid-term, and long-term complex cybersecurity R&D;
    - includes input from the private sector and academia; and
    - is consistent with the updated national cybersecurity strategy (when available).
- Identify and report shortages in researchers in the cybersecurity field to the national Cybersecurity Coordinator, which should be used to

update the national cybersecurity strategy with the appropriate plans for addressing human capital weaknesses.
- Establish a mechanism, in working with the Office of Management and Budget and consistent with existing law, to keep track of all ongoing and completed federal cybersecurity R&D projects and associated funding, to the maximum extent possible without jeopardizing national security.
- Utilize the newly established tracking mechanism to develop an ongoing process to make federal R&D information available to federal agencies and the private sector.

AGENCY COMMENTS AND OUR EVALUATION

We received written comments on a draft of this report, which were transmitted via e-mail by OSTP's Assistant Director for Information Technology R&D. We also received written comments from the Director of NIST. In addition, we received comments from a Senior Science Advisor from NSF and technical comments from the Director of the Departmental Audit Liaison from DHS, via e-mail. Additionally, representatives from DOE indicated via e-mail that they reviewed the draft report and did not have any comments. Officials from DOD and OMB did not respond to our request for comments.

The Assistant Director for Information Technology R&D from OSTP agreed with our recommendation and provided details on the office's plans and actions to address our recommendation. For example, to address the part of the recommendation to establish a comprehensive national R&D agenda, OSTP has begun updating its current 5-year plan for cybersecurity R&D. Additionally, to address the portion of the recommendation to identify and report shortages in researchers in the cybersecurity field, NITRD officials plan to provide an assessment of these shortages as part of their annual planning and review processes. The Assistant Director for Information Technology R&D also indicated that OSTP did not concur with certain findings within our report; however, he did not provide any additional information.

The Director of NIST indicated that he agreed with our recommendation. However, he stated NIST officials recommended that we make two changes to the draft report. First, the officials believe that OSTP and NITRD are coordinating research activities and working with the federal government research community to identify a research strategy that meets critical future needs in cybersecurity. We acknowledge in the report that NITRD facilitates several activities, such as hosting monthly meetings in which agencies discuss their initiatives and compiling all of its participating agencies' cybersecurity R&D efforts and budgets. We also acknowledge that NITRD hosted the National Cyber Leap Year Summit in August 2009, which aimed to bring together researchers and developers from the private and public sectors. Nevertheless, as we state in the report, NITRD is not leading agencies in a strategic direction toward a cybersecurity agenda. Second, officials requested that we add a sentence that officials from NIST believe that a prioritized research strategy is evolving and agencies will base their research agenda on this strategy and their mission needs. We acknowledge in the report that NITRD is currently working on developing a framework that focuses on three main cybersecurity R&D themes. NITRD officials expect the framework to be finalized in time for the 2012 budget submission. However, these themes do not cover all of the priorities that should be included in a national cybersecurity R&D agenda.

Regarding comments from NSF's Senior Science Advisor, she indicated that she generally agreed with our recommendation. The Senior Science Advisor and the Departmental Audit Liaison from DHS provided technical comments, which have been incorporated in the report where appropriate.

David A. Powner
Director, Information Technology
Management Issues

Gregory C. Wilshusen
Director, Information Security Issues

APPENDIX I. OBJECTIVE, SCOPE, AND METHODOLOGY

The objective of our review was to determine the key challenges to enhancing national-level cybersecurity research and development (R&D) efforts among the federal government and private companies.

To identify the key agencies involved in federal cybersecurity R&D, we researched several cybersecurity R&D-related documents, including the President's Information Technology Advisory Committee 2005 report, the Subcommittee on Networking and Information Technology Research and Development's (NITRD) Cyber Security and Information Assurance Working

Group's *2006 Federal Plan for Cyber Security and Information Assurance R&D*, the Institute for Information Infrastructure Protection 2009 Report, and the National Security and Homeland Security Councils' *Cyberspace Policy Review*. We also reviewed NITRD's *2010 Supplement to the President's Budget*, which lists key agencies that fund and conduct cybersecurity R&D, and a previous GAO report[30] to identify the agencies that provide high-level oversight. These agencies include the Departments of Defense, Energy, and Homeland Security; the National Institute of Standards and Technology; the National Science Foundation; the Office of Management and Budget; and the Office of Science and Technology Policy.

To identify private sector organizations with a major role in cybersecurity R&D, we consulted and interviewed cybersecurity experts in the information technology (IT) and communication sectors. We developed a list of companies through the membership lists of IT and communication private sector councils, which are composed of a wide range of companies that specialize in these areas. We narrowed down the list by asking each company whether they conduct cybersecurity R&D and whether they would be willing to speak to us about their cybersecurity R&D priorities, as well as their views on what role the government should be playing in the cybersecurity R&D arena. Those that responded positively to our questions consisted of 18 companies that we included in our review. We also identified 9 additional private sector and academic organizations. We selected these experts on the basis of those we have consulted in previous reviews or who were recommended to us by other experts. Additionally, we identified other academic experts from our Executive Council for Information Management and Technology, which is composed of public- and private-sector IT management experts who assist us in obtaining different perspectives on current IT management and policy issues. We included the following industry and academic entities in our review:

  Alcatel-Lucent
  AT&T
  Carnegie Mellon University
  Digital Intelligence
  Google
  IBM Corporation
  Information Security Forum
  Information Technology Sector Coordinating Council
  In-Q-Tel

Intel Corporation
Lumeta Corporation
McAfee, Inc.
Microsoft
Net Witness
Neustar
Purdue University
Oracle Corporation
Raytheon BBN Technologies
Renesys
StrongAuth, Inc.
Symantec
University at Albany, Center for Technology in Government
Verizon Business

Three of the 27 academic and private organizations asked us not to include their names in our report, and one expert was a private sector consultant who was a former director of the National Coordination Office.

To identify key challenges to enhancing national-level cybersecurity R&D efforts, we analyzed documentation, such as agencies' research plans and cybersecurity reports, and interviewed federal officials and industry experts. We then aggregated the identified challenges and validated the top challenges by asking the experts to rank the challenges in order of importance.

In addition, we analyzed relevant federal law and policy, including the National Strategy to Secure Cyberspace, the High-Performance Computing Act of 1991, the E-Government Act of 2002, the Cyber Security Research and Development Act, the Next Generation Internet Research Act of 1998, and Homeland Security Presidential Directive 7. We also reviewed prior GAO reports.

We conducted this performance audit from June 2009 to June 2010, in accordance with generally accepted government auditing standards. Those standards require that we plan and perform the audit to obtain sufficient, appropriate evidence to provide a reasonable basis for our findings and conclusions based on our audit objective. We believe that the evidence obtained provides a reasonable basis for our findings and conclusions based on our audit objective.

End Notes

[1] A vulnerability is a flaw or weakness in hardware or software that can be exploited, resulting in a violation of an implicit or explicit security policy.

[2] GAO, *High-Risk Series: An Update*, GAO-09-271 (Washington, D.C.: January 2009).

[3] Cybersecurity refers to the defense against attacks on the information technology infrastructure of an organization or, in this case, of the federal government and agencies. Cybersecurity is intertwined with the physical security of assets—from computers, networks, and their infrastructure to the environment surrounding these systems. While both parts of security are necessary to achieve overall security, this report focuses on protecting software and data from attacks that are electronic in nature and that typically arrive over a data communication link. Cybersecurity is a major concern of both the federal government and the private sector.

[4] The White House, National Security Presidential Directive 54/Homeland Security Presidential Directive 23 (Washington, D.C.: Jan. 8, 2008).

[5] GAO, *Cybersecurity: Progress Made but Challenges Remain in Defining and Coordinating the Comprehensive National Initiative*, GAO-10-338 (Washington, D.C.: Mar. 5, 2010).

[6] The *National Infrastructure Protection Plan*, which was published in 2006 and revised in 2009, defines the organizational structures that provide the framework for coordination of critical infrastructure protection efforts at all levels of government as well as within and across private-sector-specific councils. These coordinating councils are composed of the representatives of owners and operators, generally from the private sector.

[7] Examples of the problems identified by DHS include the following: scalable trustworthy systems, enterprise-level metrics, combating insider threats, global-scale identity management, situational understanding and attack attribution, privacy-aware security, and usable security.

[8] Budget figures provided to NITRD by agencies to include in its annual supplement to the President's budget do not include funding for classified R&D projects.

[9] The White House, *The National Strategy to Secure Cyberspace* (Washington, D.C.: February 2003).

[10] President's Information Technology Advisory Committee, *Cyber Security: A Crisis of Prioritization* (Arlington, Va.: Feb. 28, 2005).

[11] President's Council of Advisors on Science and Technology, *Leadership Under Challenge: Information Technology R&D in a Competitive World* (Washington, D.C.: Aug. 10, 2007).

[12] Center for Strategic and International Studies, *Securing Cyberspace for the 44th Presidency: A Report of the CSIS Commission on Cyber Security for the 44 Presidencyth* (Washington, D.C.: December 2008).

[13] The Institute for Information Infrastructure Protection is a national consortium of academic institutions, federally funded labs, and nonprofit organizations dedicated to strengthening the cyber infrastructure of the United States.

[14] The National Security Council and the Homeland Security Council, *Cyberspace Policy Review: Assuring a Trusted and Resilient Information and Communications Infrastructure* (Washington, D.C.: May 29, 2009).

[15] GAO, *Information Security: Coordination of Federal Cyber Security Research and Development*, GAO-06-811 (Washington, D.C.: Sept. 29, 2006).

[16] GAO, *National Cybersecurity Strategy: Key Improvements Are Needed to Strengthen the Nation's Posture*, GAO-09-432T (Washington, D.C.: Mar. 10, 2009).

[17] GAO-06-811.

[18] Experts from 3 of the 27 private sector organizations and academic institutions did not respond to our request to rank the challenges.

[19] See, for example, GAO, *Results-Oriented Government: Practices That Can Help Enhance and Sustain Collaboration among Federal Agencies*, GAO-06-15 (Washington, D.C.: Oct. 21,

2005); and *Internet Infrastructure: DHS Faces Challenges in Developing a Joint Public/Private Recovery Plan*, GAO-06-672 (Washington, D.C.: June 16, 2006).

[20] For more information on GAO reports and recommendations related to information sharing, see GAO, *Information Sharing: Practices That Can Benefit Critical Infrastructure Protection*, GAO-02-24 (Washington, D.C.: Oct. 15, 2001); *Critical Infrastructure Protection: Improving Information Sharing with Infrastructure Sectors*, GAO-04-780 (Washington, D.C.: July 09, 2004); *High-Risk Series: An Update*, GAO-05-207 (Washington, D.C.: January 2005); *Critical Infrastructure Protection: Department of Homeland Security Faces Challenges in Fulfilling Cybersecurity Responsibilities*, GAO-05-434 (Washington, D.C.: May 26, 2005); and *Cyber Analysis and Warning: DHS Faces Challenges in Establishing a Comprehensive National Capability*, GAO-08-588 (Washington, D.C.: July 31, 2008).

[21] The IT-SCC R&D working group's proposal consists of establishing a repeatable process in which the private sector and government would, among other things, identify gaps between R&D initiatives and priorities in the public and private sectors. The gap analysis would be developed by both sectors sharing their current R&D activities; infrastructure risks, threats, and vulnerabilities; and known conditions (e.g., integrity of software code and pieces of the infrastructure that are not inherently secure). It was proposed that this work would result in a published document that would articulate R&D priorities and a roadmap and would be updated on a regular basis.

[22] GAO-06-811.

[23] DOD's National Cyber Range is a testing environment for cybersecurity researchers to assist in producing qualitative and quantitative assessments of various cybersecurity technologies and scenarios. This was developed under CNCI.

[24] 15 U.S.C. § 740 1(5)(B).

[25] The INFOSEC Research Council consists of government sponsors of information security research from DOD, the intelligence community, and federal civil agencies. The council aims to provide its membership with a communitywide forum to discuss critical information security issues, convey the research needs of their respective communities, and describe current research initiatives and proposed courses of action for future research investments.

[26] INFOSEC Research Council, *Hard Problems List* (November 2005).

[27] *Securing Cyberspace for the 44th Presidency: A Report of the CSIS Commission*

[28] Pub. L. No. 107-347, § 207(g)(1)(A), 116 Stat. 2899, 2919-21 (Dec. 17, 2002).

[29] GAO-06-811.

[30] GAO, *Information Security: Coordination of Federal Cyber Security Research and Development*, GAO-06-811 (Washington, D.C.: Sept. 29, 2006).

INDEX

A

access, viii, 6, 65, 68
accessibility, 69
accountability, 7, 8, 12, 13, 53, 56
accreditation, 47
administrative support, 71, 73
administrators, 6
advancement, 84, 85
agencies, vii, viii, 1, 2, 3, 4, 5, 7, 8, 10, 13, 14, 15, 16, 17, 18, 19, 21, 22, 23, 24, 26, 27, 28, 29, 30, 31, 32, 33, 35, 36, 37, 39, 43, 45, 46, 47, 48, 49, 50, 51, 53, 54, 56, 57, 58, 59, 60, 61, 62, 65, 66, 69, 70, 71, 72, 73, 75, 76, 77, 78, 79, 80, 81, 82, 83, 84, 86, 88, 89, 90, 92, 93, 94
agency initiatives, 36
Air Force, 75
America COMPETES Act, 73, 74, 79
annual review, 62, 74
architect, 18, 38, 41
assessment, 35, 41, 48, 49, 73, 89
assets, 5, 31, 40, 41, 92
AT&T, 91
attacker, 76
attribution, 93
audit, 5, 7, 13, 56, 60, 69, 92
authorities, 11, 24, 26, 27, 61
authority, 24, 26, 27, 28, 34, 37, 41, 45, 48, 56, 61
awareness, 35, 36, 40, 41, 42, 46, 62

B

barriers, 8, 22
base, 86, 90
behaviors, 11
benefits, 32, 54, 69
Bush, President, 62
business function, 38, 40

C

candidates, 22, 23, 24, 25, 62
capital account, 8
career development, 11
cation, 41
certificate, 32
certification, 32, 33, 34, 47, 55
CFR, 61, 62
challenges, viii, 2, 4, 5, 6, 7, 12, 17, 22, 23, 25, 29, 51, 53, 56, 60, 65, 66, 69, 70, 79, 80, 87, 88, 90, 92, 93
Chief of Staff, 55
classification, 31
collaboration, 19, 41, 74, 86, 87

colleges, 22, 86
commercial, 34, 70, 76, 84
communication, 91, 93
community, 36, 44, 71, 75, 89, 94
compensation, 2, 8, 23, 30, 31, 51
competition, 23
complexity, 2, 24, 81, 87
compliance, 13, 16, 38
computer, 6, 7, 23, 38, 68, 69, 81
computing, 85
conference, 67
confidentiality, 5
configuration, 41
Congress, 29, 61, 62, 71, 86
consensus, 23, 37, 45
contractor workforce, vii, 1, 6
cooperation, 43
coordination, 2, 11, 42, 47, 51, 53, 66, 67, 70, 72, 73, 74, 75, 77, 78, 87, 93
cost, 32, 51
credentials, 21, 39, 45
crimes, 44
critical infrastructure, 6, 70, 93
curriculum, 33
customers, 76
cybersecurity, vii, viii, 1, 2, 3, 4, 6, 7, 8, 10, 11, 12, 13, 14, 15, 16, 17, 18, 19, 20, 21, 22, 23, 24, 26, 27, 28, 29, 30, 31, 32, 33, 34, 35, 36, 37, 39, 42, 43, 44, 45, 46, 47, 48, 50, 51, 52, 53, 54, 55, 56, 57, 58, 59, 60, 65, 66, 67, 69, 70, 72, 73, 74, 75, 76, 77, 78, 79, 80, 81, 82, 83, 84, 85, 86, 87, 88, 89, 90, 91, 92, 94
cybersecurity personnel, vii, 1, 2, 4, 7, 10, 17, 23, 24, 26, 28, 31, 32, 33, 51, 58, 59
cybersecurity staff, vii, 1, 7, 14, 20, 22, 23, 59
cyberspace, 66, 77, 79, 85

D

data collection, 14, 16

data communication, 93
data gathering, 15, 29, 59
database, 68, 86, 87
deficiencies, 56
Department of Commerce, 3, 7, 61
Department of Defense, 2, 3, 61, 67
Department of Education, 36
Department of Energy, 67
Department of Health and Human Services, 3, 55
Department of Homeland Security, 3, 54, 67, 93
Department of Justice, 4, 7
Department of the Treasury, 4, 55
Department of Transportation, 3, 55, 76
DHS, 3, 5, 7, 10, 11, 15, 20, 22, 23, 25, 27, 28, 30, 33, 34, 35, 36, 37, 44, 45, 46, 47, 48, 49, 50, 51, 56, 57, 58, 61, 67, 69, 70, 72, 73, 75, 76, 78, 79, 80, 81, 85, 87, 89, 90, 93
digital evidence, 44
distribution, 54
DOT, 3, 5, 10, 12, 15, 20, 23, 25, 27, 33, 34, 59
draft, 29, 34, 35, 37, 39, 44, 54, 55, 57, 62, 89

E

education, 2, 11, 32, 34, 35, 36, 62, 71, 75, 85
E-Government Act, 61, 72, 86, 92
e-mail, 56, 89
employees, 6, 8, 9, 10, 11, 12, 14, 15, 16, 17, 18, 22, 24, 25, 27, 28, 29, 30, 31, 32, 34, 42, 46, 47, 59, 61, 85
employment, 26, 27, 28, 50
employment programs, 26, 27, 28
encryption, 76
enforcement, 16, 19, 38
engineering, 16, 36, 38, 73, 75
environment, 35, 38, 38, 46, 75, 85, 92, 94

Environmental Protection Agency, 74
espionage, 6
essay question, 25
evidence, 5, 11, 13, 22, 23, 24, 38, 44, 60, 69, 82, 92
execution, 32
executive branch, 62
Executive Order, 71
exercise, 66, 88
expertise, 7, 86
exploitation, 19

F

FBI, 3, 21, 22, 26, 28, 33
FDA, 62
federal agency, 36, 87
Federal Bureau of Investigation, (FBI), 3, 21, 61
federal government, viii, 3, 7, 31, 34, 35, 42, 43, 45, 50, 65, 66, 68, 69, 77, 78, 82, 83, 84, 85, 89, 90, 92
Federal Government, 62
federal hiring, 2, 24
federal IT infrastructure, vii, 1, 4
federal law, 65, 69, 92
federal workforce, 34, 37, 51
financial, 6, 50, 51
financial system, 6
fiscal year 2009, 59
flexibility, 26, 30
focus groups, 42
force, 9, 19
foreign policy, 71
formation, 72
foundations, 81
fraud, 68, 69
funding, 20, 23, 34, 35, 66, 67, 76, 79, 84, 86, 87, 88, 93
funds, 28, 32, 76, 83

G

GAO, vii, viii, 1, 2, 9, 10, 15, 16, 23, 25, 27, 31, 33, 36, 38, 42, 56, 58, 59, 60, 61, 62, 63, 65, 66, 74, 78, 90, 92, 93, 94
General Services Administration, 76
governance, 37, 53, 56
governmentwide cybersecurity workforce initiatives, vii, 1, 5, 53, 58, 60
grades, 30, 31
graduate students, 50
grants, 76, 84
group identity, 43
growth, 85
guidance, 15, 20, 21, 29, 36, 39, 51, 53, 57, 59, 76, 78, 80, 86
guidelines, 2, 11, 18, 19, 20, 45, 57, 59, 76

H

Health and Human Services, 3, 5, 52, 55, 59
HHS, 3, 5, 10, 13, 15, 19, 22, 23, 25, 27, 28, 33, 59
hiring, 2, 7, 11, 12, 13, 21, 22, 23, 24, 25, 26, 28, 31, 51, 59, 61, 62
House, 61, 68, 77, 93
House of Representatives, 68
human, 8, 9, 10, 11, 12, 13, 14, 30, 31, 36, 52, 54, 55, 57, 59, 85, 86, 88
human capital, 8, 9, 10, 11, 12, 13, 14, 30, 31, 52, 54, 55, 57, 59, 85, 86, 88
human resources, 36, 60

I

ICE, 45
identification, 11, 17, 36
identity, 6, 43, 81, 93
improvements, viii, 17, 31, 58, 65, 69, 75, 76, 78, 80
independence, 21

individuals, 6, 24, 26, 27, 32, 40, 41, 44, 46, 68, 69
industry, 16, 67, 69, 71, 73, 83, 84, 91, 92
information sharing, 83, 93
information technology, vii, 1, 3, 4, 11, 16, 58, 67, 71, 73, 77, 91, 92
infrastructure, vii, 1, 4, 6, 7, 19, 72, 85, 88, 92, 93, 94
institutions, viii, 65, 69, 71, 93
integration, 41
integrity, 5, 43, 94
intellectual property, 6, 83
intelligence, 14, 15, 44, 50, 70, 71, 94
Internal Revenue Service, 27, 28
investments, 32, 73, 75, 76, 84, 94
issues, 11, 12, 13, 38, 43, 71, 80, 81, 91, 94

materials, 39
mathematics, 36
mathematics education, 36
matrix, 39
measurement, 53
medical, 6
membership, 32, 73, 91, 94
mentoring program, 33
methodology, 5, 57, 69
Microsoft, 91
military, 7, 32, 50, 75
mission, 7, 8, 9, 11, 12, 18, 20, 21, 30, 35, 75, 76, 90
missions, 5, 26, 28, 34, 40, 41, 47, 66, 79
models, 9, 11, 21, 34, 41, 46, 57

J

justification, 13

K

kindergarten, 36

L

law enforcement, 19
lead, 21, 45, 82
leadership, 11, 66, 71, 73, 82, 87, 88
learning, 39
life cycle, 38

M

magnitude, 40
majority, 2, 15, 87
malware, 23
management, 5, 7, 9, 10, 11, 12, 13, 14, 16, 18, 19, 30, 31, 35, 38, 41, 49, 59, 62, 81, 85, 91, 93

N

National Aeronautics and Space Administration, 4, 35, 74
National Economic Council, 71
National Institutes of Health, 74
national security, 4, 7, 71, 87, 88
National Security Agency, 4, 22, 28, 67, 72, 73, 75
National Security Council, 71, 72, 93
National Strategy, 66, 77, 79, 84, 86, 92, 93
national-level cybersecurity, viii, 65, 69, 90, 92
negotiating, 28
networking, 71, 77, 81
nonprofit organizations, 93
NSA, 4, 22, 28, 30, 32, 36, 50, 67, 72, 73, 74, 75

O

Obama, President, viii, 4, 24, 60, 65, 69, 78
Office of Management and Budget, 3, 4, 5, 53, 59, 66, 68, 69, 72, 88, 91
Office of the Inspector General, 61

officials, viii, 3, 12, 13, 17, 19, 20, 21, 22, 23, 24, 25, 28, 30, 31, 32, 33, 34, 35, 36, 37, 40, 43, 45, 47, 48, 56, 59, 60, 65, 66, 71, 75, 76, 80, 81, 82, 83, 84, 85, 86, 87, 89, 92
OMB, 4, 5, 13, 14, 15, 17, 46, 56, 57, 59, 60, 61, 68, 69, 70, 72, 73, 78, 80, 86, 89
operations, 5, 6, 12, 18, 19, 38, 39, 40, 41, 60, 68, 69
opportunities, 29, 51, 54, 74, 87
organ, 37
organize, 82
outreach, 22
overlap, 3, 47
oversight, 13, 29, 70, 75, 77, 78, 87, 90

P

parallel, 74
participants, 3, 18, 32, 35, 48, 54, 74
pipeline, 22, 36, 77
planned action, 66
playing, 82, 91
policy, 19, 20, 28, 32, 69, 71, 72, 77, 91, 92
policy issues, 91
population, 35
portfolio, 77
preservation, 38
President, viii, 4, 24, 25, 60, 62, 65, 68, 69, 70, 71, 72, 73, 74, 77, 78, 84, 90, 93
President Obama, viii, 4, 24, 65, 69, 78
principles, 9, 10, 38, 51, 59
private sector, viii, 23, 36, 44, 65, 66, 67, 69, 71, 74, 76, 78, 79, 81, 82, 83, 84, 85, 87, 88, 89, 91, 92, 93, 94
procurement, 41
professional development, 12, 36
professionals, 6, 7, 21, 24, 26, 28, 36, 42, 45, 50, 62, 85
profit, 83, 84
project, 11, 21, 83
proposed regulations, 29

protection, 4, 93
public awareness, 36
public sector, 83, 84, 89
publishing, 73

Q

qualifications, 27, 28, 31, 39

R

R&D investments, 76, 84
recognition, 11
recommendations, iv, 2, 31, 35, 51, 54, 56, 58, 74, 76, 77, 78, 79, 80, 93
recruiting, vii, 1, 7, 8, 11, 12, 13, 21, 22, 23, 27, 28, 29, 30, 31, 50
reform, 17, 25, 30, 31
regulations, 29, 62
reliability, 81
requirements, 2, 10, 11, 12, 13, 14, 32, 40, 41, 42, 52, 55, 57
research and development (R&D), viii, 65, 69, 90
researchers, 67, 84, 85, 86, 87, 88, 89, 94
resources, 5, 6, 35, 36, 37, 46, 51, 53, 54, 60
response, 18, 19, 25, 38, 43
retention rate, 50, 54, 58
rewards, 7
risk, 4, 5, 6, 18, 26, 38, 40, 41, 42, 47, 66, 67, 68, 70, 75, 77, 81, 84, 87
risks, 36, 38, 40, 88, 94
rules, 7, 62

S

sabotage, 69
scholarship, 26
science, 16, 36, 70, 71, 72, 73, 75, 80
scope, 5, 29, 58, 69
Secretary of Commerce, 52, 53, 54, 56
Secretary of Defense, 10, 52, 54, 76

Secretary of Homeland Security, 53
security, 4, 5, 6, 7, 10, 11, 12, 13, 14, 15, 16, 18, 20, 21, 22, 23, 24, 25, 33, 34, 38, 39, 40, 41, 42, 44, 46, 49, 50, 51, 60, 62, 66, 68, 70, 71, 75, 76, 79, 81, 84, 85, 87, 88, 92, 93, 94
security threats, 38
services, 5, 6, 17, 46, 47, 50, 81
SFS, 4, 50
shortage, 7, 23, 85
skilled personnel, 7, 28
skilled workers, 36, 85
Social Security, 6
software, 18, 38, 39, 43, 92, 94
software code, 94
solution, 41
specialists, 42, 85
spending, 29, 58, 87
Spring, 73, 74
stakeholders, 8, 9, 10
states, 6, 11, 12, 21, 28, 35, 36, 89
strategic planning, 37, 60
structure, 3, 13, 21, 35, 37, 53, 56, 60
supervisors, 11, 24, 25

T

talent, 3, 8, 11, 21, 22, 26
target, 38, 55, 56
technical comments, 58, 89, 90
techniques, 40, 69
technologies, 75, 94
technology, vii, 1, 2, 3, 4, 11, 16, 36, 38, 58, 67, 68, 70, 71, 72, 73, 75, 77, 80, 83, 86, 91, 92
testing, 23, 38, 75, 94
Thompson, Bennie G., 68
threats, 7, 38, 44, 51, 62, 70, 75, 77, 80, 93, 94
time frame, 20, 34, 37, 45, 81
Title I, II, 61

tracks, 13, 43, 67, 77, 87
training, 2, 3, 7, 8, 11, 12, 13, 15, 17, 18, 19, 20, 21, 25, 31, 32, 33, 34, 35, 36, 37, 40, 41, 42, 43, 45, 46, 47, 48, 49, 51, 54, 59, 60, 62, 85, 86
training programs, 31, 32, 33, 34, 47
Treasury, 4, 5, 10, 13, 15, 17, 20, 21, 23, 25, 27, 28, 30, 33, 34, 52, 55, 59, 72, 74

U

United, v, viii, 1, 4, 7, 35, 65, 68, 70, 85, 87, 93
United States, v, viii, 1, 4, 7, 35, 65, 68, 70, 85, 87, 93
universities, 22, 86
updating, 53, 57, 74, 77, 78, 85, 89

V

validation, 19
Verizon, 92
vision, 35
vulnerability, 18, 38, 92

W

Washington, 5, 60, 61, 62, 63, 92, 93, 94
weakness, 92
White House, 61, 77, 93
workers, 14, 28, 29, 36, 50, 51, 85
workforce, vii, 1, 2, 3, 4, 6, 7, 8, 9, 10, 11, 12, 13, 14, 15, 16, 17, 19, 20, 21, 27, 32, 34, 35, 36, 37, 39, 43, 44, 45, 46, 47, 48, 49, 50, 51, 52, 53, 54, 55, 56, 57, 58, 59, 60, 85
working groups, 36, 62, 70, 72, 74
workload, 18